YOUNG, BROKE & EDUCATED

A Discussion of Millennials, Finance, Economics and Poverty

by
ALEXANDER BAIMA

FROM THE TINY ACORN …
GROWS THE MIGHTY OAK

Young, Broke & Educated
Copyright © 2020 Alexander Baima. All rights reserved.
Printed in the United States of America. For information, address
Acorn Publishing, LLC, 3943 Irvine Blvd. Ste. 218, Irvine, CA 92602

www.acornpublishingllc.com

Interior design and formatting by Debra Cranfield Kennedy

ISBN-13: 978-1-952112-08-9 (hardcover)
ISBN-13: 978-1-952112-07-2 (paperback)
LCCN: 2020911960

Biography

Alexander Baima received his bachelor's degree in Business Administration from the University of San Diego. By profession, he has excelled as both an analyst and a project manager. He currently holds a CAPM, MOS and SSGB certification in the field of project management. Alex is a talented entrepreneur who specializes in 19th and 20th century porcelain as well as modern innovative computing.

Alex is a firm supporter of Cryptocurrency and believes that this technology will revolutionize the way all countries function within a matter of a few years. He is currently invested in Bitcoin, Ethereum and EOS with the expectations that decentralized applications and smart contracts will be a major contributor to our future.

He has published over 150 articles between LinkedIn and a new social media platform called Steemit. As a millennial, his desire is to help solve many of the great challenges that are plaguing today's society and engage in intellectual exchanges to help create a better world.

Acknowledgments

I would like to thank Glen Davenport and Nick Saba. Your support, suggestions, direction and insight helped make this book the very best that it could be. I also wanted to thank everyone who has supported me during this project. I dedicate this book to all the young people in America who want change.

Preface

I remember going to the computer lab when I was in the second grade and playing one of my favorite games, SimCity 2000. It was an original idea at the time where someone could plan, budget and build an entire city. SimCity 2000 was made by a man named Will Wright who cofounded Maxis games and created titles such as SimCity, The Sims and SimAnt. I remember thinking, *how could one person be responsible for three of the greatest games I had ever played?*

One of the things I remember most was that on the SimCity 2000 disc was an interview with Will Wright. In this interview Will stated "the best games I've seen were designed by people designing them for themselves." I wrote this book because it was something I wanted to read, yet, I couldn't find it anywhere.

A challenge America is facing is that many members of older generations have lost the ability to recognize change. They see the same version of America that they grew up with, but the truth is that America has changed significantly in quite a short time. At the same time many people get lost in emotion and have a hard time seeing logic and reason. They often want to blame somebody or something so they can relinquish personal responsibility. This is why this book is written with facts, math, statistics and research sources believed to be credible. It's time that someone reintroduced mathematical reasoning into the world.

This book is broken up into three main sections. Each chapter explores an economic, financial or social issue. Later chapters bring together previous chapters to make arguments and predictions of future events and how they could unfold.

The first section of this book looks at the finances and history of the past several generations. The main focus of this section is how and why newer generations have less purchasing power in comparison to previous generations. I want to give the world an understanding of the challenges that the average young person is now experiencing in America. Chapters in this section talk about how everyday costs and excessive debt are making it harder for young people to save money and how this is affecting their lives. This section explains the new habits that younger people are developing to react to these increased costs and why concepts of inflation are inaccurate. This section also demonstrates how the standard of living previous generations experienced is unsustainable and that newer generations need to work twice as hard to have the same lifestyle as their parents.

The second section of this book looks at the systems that govern America, how these systems have changed over time, and the dependency that Americans have on them. Chapters in this block explain the problems with higher education and minimum wage, and offer possible solutions to improve them. This section explains why the middle class is dwindling and how modern hiring in America by corporations is leading to a larger population of poor people. This section analyzes the shifts in population dynamics and government finances. It explains how previously passed legislation is forcing higher taxes on young people to buy time for the inevitable failing of government programs such as social security, welfare and pensions. This section highlights the risk to our society being caused by mis-management of our financial and banking systems.

The third section of this book looks at the wealth distribution in America and aims to explain what will happen when the debt and credit bubble bursts. This section analyzes the inevitability of wealth redistribution and looks at how socialism, debt forgiveness, or the introduction of cryptocurrency might be able to solve this problem. This section unveils why the United States and world are set to evolve, and how in only a few short years the dollar will no longer exist in its present form. This section also talks about possible investments that might be a good choice to preserve wealth, even in a time where many people could lose everything. For a long time, Americans and the government have been living beyond their means. There will be repercussions resulting from this carelessness.

I want this book to spark awareness and action, and teach the truths that were ignored in the education system. Many millennials went to college and took on a boatload of debt in the hope that they could have a lifestyle resembling the one experienced by their parents. But instead of graduating and receiving the great jobs they were promised, many millennials are trapped living paycheck to paycheck and are caught in an endless loop to pay for their most basic needs. The purchasing power of newer generations is lower and their quality of life is declining. But when did this happen, and how did we get here? When did we leave the great utopia that our grandparents talked about and enter an age where many millennials are stuck living with their parents into their mid 30s? How can we get back to that utopia? This book reveals how we can interrupt this cycle and break new ground. I also discuss the challenges and sacrifices that need to be made so that once again young people will have the opportunities that made America a place that people dream about.

I hope *Young, Broke and Educated* creates a willingness to not just tackle something new, but advocate for something new.

This book provides reference points using math to show how much the U.S. has changed over the past few generations. Most of this book uses data and statistics from 2015 to 2019 and compares this information to data and statistics from the 1990s. This is done for several reasons. Firstly, the 90s were considered a time that the economy was doing well. Secondly, many statistics provided by the Social Security Administration, Census Bureau, other government agencies and independent researchers tend to be about 1½ to 2 years behind real time. Where it is possible, I have used the most current statistics available.

When writing *Young, Broke and Educated*, I tried to use median statistics and not averages when possible. Unfortunately, medians are not available for many statistics, in which case averages will be used. An average is taking the product of everyone and dividing it equally, the median is the number where half the population does better, half does worse. For example, if 9 people make 0 dollars a year and 1 person makes $1,000,000, the average is $100,000. The median on the other hand would be 0 dollars. Using medians for incomes prevents inaccurate and overinflated numbers caused by super earners like Bill Gates or Jeff Bezos. Using medians for real estate removes $100,000,000 mansions in Hollywood from the equation. In general, averages tend to be higher than that of medians and thus give a skewed representation of reality.

At its core, this book is a cross between finance and economics. These two subjects are heavily reliant on the understanding of causality and how supply, demand, and incentives affect human behavior. In economics classes they teach you about supply and demand using clean little diagrams with straight lines that show as prices go up, demand goes down.

Real economics is messy and doesn't work with straight lines; for instance, some people choose not to buy goods at extremely low prices, often because they perceive them to be of lower quality. Although there are many buyers that seek the lowest price, there are also many buyers who seek the highest quality product. For them, price is of little importance.

Economics classes often talk about the demand curve and how it can be shifted with events, but they never go into detail about these events, about what causes them, or how stock prices can soar or crash because of them. A single FDA approval for an up-and-coming pharmaceutical company can send stock prices soaring and a rejection from the FDA to a company without other drug prospects can bankrupt them.

Economics classes never teach you how diplomatic decisions made by different countries can affect a market. When China boycotted coal from North Korea in 2017 it increased the demand of U.S. mined coal and helped create a market boom. These are examples of how short-term events can greatly affect a market. To truly gain a grasp of economics, one must become a great detective and a dedicated tracker of world news.

Almost every resource on the planet has a fluctuation of value based on supply and demand. If prices start to shoot much higher, more companies will enter a given market, and if prices collapse many companies in that industry will experience financial difficulties and may even go out of business. This often leads to events that have a big impact on the economy, but take many years to be fully realized. One such example is how the voting, overspending and irresponsibility of previous generations has led to a financial struggle and decreased quality of life for millennials and young people growing up today.

Young, Broke and Educated is for the people who are hungry for logic, reason and economics. It is for the millennials who are tired of not getting their voice heard, as well as for those open to hearing and sharing ideas. As someone who has little free time, I intend this to be a short and manageable book to read, and not some intimidating three-inch-thick monster that will take you months to finish and make you run away crying. I hope you enjoy the book.

YOUNG,
BROKE &
EDUCATED

————

Table of Contents

THE CHALLENGES YOUNG PEOPLE FACE AND HOW WE GOT HERE

CHAPTER 1

Bridging the Generation Gap

For the last 150 years or so, parents of each generation have had the simple goal of providing a better quality of life for their children than they experienced. The millennials are the first generation in this modern era in which the majority of Americans expect they will have a lower quality of life than the generation that preceded them.

Suicide has surged to the highest level in nearly 30 years,[1] and between 1988 and 2008, America experienced a 400% increase in the use of antidepressants.[2] Children are now being raised in daycare, by strangers, and by their electronic devices more than by their actual parents.

In an age where young people experience being "triggered" and needing "safe spaces," and when century-old confederate monuments are now being branded as hateful and being torn down, someone has to ask, *What on earth is going on?* Throughout history, we have always experienced times where there were great periods of change, but we are perhaps experiencing some of the biggest changes today. In addition to evolving technology and differing attitudes, the past 50 years also created and separated the richest and the poorest generations in American history. This generational wealth gap will be fueling most of the changes in America driving forward, as well as most of the discussion in this book.

I grew up in what most would call an upper middle class family. When I was young, both my father and mother worked full-time jobs, and then later, my father became the sole income provider. Every year my parents and grandparents would go on lavish vacations to exotic destinations where they would spend a week enjoying an amazing experience. Almost weekly, my parents would dine at high quality restaurants, buy expensive jewelry and live a relatively grandiose lifestyle. I was programmed along with millions of other millennials that if I went to college and worked hard, this would be my life too. Six years removed from college at the age of 29, I had never been on a vacation, and I still considered In-N-Out a high quality dining establishment. When my parents were 29, they already owned their first house.

Unfortunately, in most discussions about generations, many of us receive only the viewpoints of older people who are generally more financially established and are the primary consumers of luxury services in America. Business owners and the media are more prone to represent only these consumers, limiting their focus on their most profitable customers. When you see millennials getting upset about the unequal distribution of wealth, this is one of the reasons why. I aim to provide a view from their side.

I graduated college in 2012 with a four-year liberal arts degree in business administration from what was said to be one of the top 25 business schools in America. Truth was, I never wanted to go to college, but like many young people in America, I endured significant pressure from just about everyone. How many times in your life have you seen a TV commercial telling you not to go to college? Like many, I was told that if I didn't get a college degree, I would never amount to much of anything. The plan was that I would go to college, make tons of money, and live happily ever after in a mansion overlooking the beach. At least, this was what the commercials, the college itself, and my parents suggested would be the reality.

My first job out of college started as an unpaid internship, even though I had already had an unpaid internship during my senior year of college. This would eventually turn into a minimum wage job. I commuted over two hours a day to work at a company where I acted as broker support and made retirement packages for people who were retiring from fortune 500 companies. While I was poor as hell, the brokers I was servicing were making a seven-figure incomes.

After almost a year of this, I got a job that I thought would be heaven-sent. Less than a week after I arrived, I received a pink slip for corporate layoffs that would affect over 7,000 people. For the next few years I bounced around between different jobs, working for temp agencies and contract companies, feeling like I was going nowhere. I realized I wasn't alone as I saw many people I knew were in similar situations.

Chances are if you're a millennial, you've been struggling. If you've been struggling, you've probably heard the story. You know, the one told by middle-aged people. The story generally starts with the storyteller telling you about a time 50 years ago when they came to America on a leaky boat with only $50 in their pocket. The story eventually ends after an hour of drama and reaches the conclusion that you're struggling because you haven't worked hard enough. These same people make comments about how expensive milk has become when they walk into a supermarket. They act so surprised that milk is now $4, as if it just tripled in price in the last few days. With inflation slowly eroding away the purchasing power of the dollar, many people simply don't see the changes in their everyday life. Most of the older generations simply refuse to acknowledge the amazing opportunities and wealth that their generation experienced and that times have changed drastically in the last several decades.

As a member of a newer and more troubled generation I am

often deep in thought about one question. What is the American dream, and how has it changed? Is it the opportunity for prosperity, success or freedom? Can anything be achieved through hard work, regardless of birth circumstances? Everyone is going to have a somewhat different answer to what the American dream is. My dream is to own a house, and not have a mortgage. However, in today's economy, is it even possible for a millennial to buy a house and own it outright? In the 50s and 60s one person working as a fry cook made enough money to afford rent, and a man with a decent job could support a stay-at-home wife and a child. Why has owning a house or renting become such a challenge for millennials when it was so easy for previous generations?

At the heart of modern America are the two largest and most influential generations in society. Ironically these two generations are at different times in their lives and have drastically different views and opinions. It is important to understand these different generations, as they are ultimately playing tug of war to shape the future of America. I am talking about the baby boomers and the millennials.

The baby boomers were a product of one of the hardest working generations in history. This generation that preceded them was known as The Silent Generation. The Silent Generation was comprised of individuals born between 1928 and 1946. Members of this generation typically worked far in excess of 40 hours a week, were not paid overtime, and often found themselves in poor quality factory conditions. It wasn't until 1940 when congress ratified the Fair Labor Standards Act, under which workweeks would be reduced to 40 hours and employers would be required to pay overtime to employees who worked more than 44 hours a week. It was ultimately The Silent Generation or the parents of the baby boomers who built some of the greatest buildings and created some of the strongest lasting effects on society in the United States.

Baby boomers, born between 1946 and 1964 were unique in the fact that unlike many of the previous generations, they did not grow up in a time of great turbulence or financial difficulty. There was no life changing recession like the one that occurred in 1929. The economy was thriving and WWI and WWII were already over. The United States held its final military draft in 1973 for the Vietnam War, in which few baby boomers would see the battlefield. For the majority of the baby boomers, the largest challenge they would face was the oil crisis in the 1970s. While their youth years may have been challenging like that of every other generation, they received more support and financial advantages in comparison to generations preceding and succeeding them.

One advantage the baby boomers experienced was a better labor market and fewer job requirements. Many baby boomers generally worked one or several jobs in their lifetime and received a gold watch after 35 to 40 years of service. Millennials are struggling to find a job that lasts 1 or 2 years. For members of newer generations, working more than ten years at the same place today is almost unheard of.

In today's labor market, many people have become thankful to just have a job, and thus do not engage in negotiation of wages or move to other companies. This is leading to many younger workers being exploited and deliberately kept at low wages. In addition, there are greater barriers to entry for millennials seeking high quality jobs in comparison to what previous generations needed to go through. My father became a fish and game warden in the 1970s with a high school degree. Today this position generally requires an associate degree in natural resource science or criminal justice.

Another advantage baby boomers experienced was the explosive growth of the stock market. Their generation witnessed the Dow Jones

Industrial Average increase from approximately 200 in 1950 to almost 30,000 in 2019, a growth of 1500x. For those who chose to invest, this was life changing.

Many members of the baby boomers and the silent generation were able to buy houses at a young age and experienced astronomical capital gains on their property. My grandparents bought a house in San Francisco in the early 1970s for less than $25,000. The average person in 1970 made roughly $6,200 a year. If we excluded taxes and said that someone could save half their income, a single person could afford to pay off a mortgage in eight years. Today the house that my grandparents bought is worth approximately $900,000. A person today would need to make over $220,000 per year to pay off that mortgage in eight years. A millennial is unlikely to earn the $220,000 income needed to buy what their grandparents bought for a normal $6,200 middle class income. Is it realistic to think that millennials will see this same appreciation in housing prices? How did this real estate price boom happen?

While for many decades America was seen as the land of opportunity, with today's debt we risk moving closer towards a caste system like that of India where the class you are born into is the class you stay in your entire life. Younger people are becoming increasingly reliant on their parents and grandparents to help them pay off college debt, and housing they could not afford.

Many angry millennials only see one side of the coin when looking at wealthy Americans. To them, the rich are bloodsucking leeches who have made their money by screwing over young people or foreigners. They do not see these people as those who have created great products, or provide an excellent service through hard work, dedication, and education. The reality is, most of these millennials were prey of higher education and bank loan systems that put them into such financial misery that these feelings are not surprising. In today's economy we are seeing a compression of companies in industries and the rise of powerful oligopolies that have a tight stranglehold over the prices of many everyday needs.

It's extremely difficult, if not outright impossible for the millennials to have the quality lifestyle that the last few generations experienced. While these economic conditions do not give someone the excuse to stop trying, they do hold weight. At what point do wages and purchasing power become so low that there is a push back from the millennials in the form of a revolution?

If in the short term we have a majority of an entire generation of people living off Top Ramen, and low-quality particle board furniture, how exactly do we get to the long term where young people are successful, own houses and start families? The millennials are at least ten years behind their parents in terms of their ability to buy and pay off a house, and many of them are still living with their parents into their early thirties. A 2016 study by Bloomberg shows the U.S. homeownership rate as the lowest since 1965,[3] and it shows no signs of getting better. It's quite clear that costs are simply too high and there is too much burden being placed on younger people in America.

As America moves forward it is becoming increasingly important to understand the differences between the baby boomers and the millennials and how their actions influence America. As the baby boomers die off, the millennials will have an increasingly greater role in determining which direction our country will take. Millennials will in all likelihood lead us down a decidedly different path than the one that the baby boomers would have selected.

CHAPTER 2

The Decline of Purchasing Power

There seems to be a set of implied expectations, or blueprints as I would call them, which are handed down by each generation. These blueprints are generally introduced by parents or grandparents and are further reinforced through television, schooling, and the media. Furthermore, many of the people who passed along this set of blueprints tend to use their own life and achievements as milestones for the next generation. Their idea is that you work hard in high school to get into a good college. You then graduate college and get a great job. After you achieve this, you get married somewhere in your mid-twenties, and have your first child. Then you buy a house in your late twenties and live happily ever after, while you continue to merrily work until you retire at the age of 63.

However, more and more millennials, as stated in the previous chapter, are staying with their parents into their late twenties and even their early thirties. Yet, the unspoken expectation is for them to be homeowners and parents. This leads parents and grandparents to question the work ethic of millennials, and millennials to question where they went wrong. Are these unwritten expectations of young people rational in today's day and age? What is causing millennials to fall short of these expectations? Are they the problem, or are things getting harder for young people in America?

Many older generations argue that things are not proportionately more expensive today than they were in years past, and that higher prices are simply a result of inflation. Due to price changes happening over a long period of time, it can be difficult to notice how much more expensive something has become. The question to ask is whether an item has become more expensive because of inflation or something else?

Inflation and deflation are two concepts that revolve around monetary supply. A decrease in the supply of money or financial notes that can be exchanged for money is known as deflation. This can sometimes occur through bank failures, but has been very rare in the 21st century. On the other hand, inflation is the opposite of deflation and is in fact extremely common. When countries decide to print more money, some resort to using the government and others use a central bank. In the United States our central bank is called the Federal Reserve. When an entity prints more money the value of said money tends to be worth less, and the costs of goods and services will increase proportionately.

Many people have it in their mind that inflation is a perfect or near perfect representation of the economy. A large number of Americans assume that if inflation rises 3%, the costs of all goods and services will also rise exactly 3%. This is not true. There are many items that have far outpaced inflation and are in fact proportionately more expensive than what previous generations had to pay for them. But how much more expensive are these goods and services? Just how much less purchasing power do people have today in comparison to 20, 30 or 50 years ago? People can argue with their opinions all day long, but they cannot refute hard mathematical proof.

This chapter will focus on inflation and use the Consumer Price Index (CPI) inflation calculator to compare past and present prices.

The CPI inflation calculator examines the weighted average of consumer goods and services and is a ballpark estimate of inflationary goods. When I say something is twice or three times as expensive, I am referring to its inflation adjusted value using the Consumer Price Index (CPI) inflation calculator. For those who are confused, this means that the price of a good or service is taken from a time period in the past and converted into today's dollars using inflation. This inflation-adjusted price estimation is then compared to the actual price of this good or service.

According to Statista, the U.S. city average for one pound of sliced bacon in December 1995, was $2.17. Adjusted for inflation from the 1995 cost, the bacon should cost about $3.49 when adjusted to 2017 dollars (using the CPI inflation calculator). In December 2017, the actual average price for the same pound of sliced bacon was $5.63.[4]

In this example we would divide the price of what the bacon was in 2017, ($5.63) by the inflation adjusted 1995 price ($3.49). In this case we discover bacon was about 61.3 % more expensive in 2017, than it was proportionately in 1995. Although not everything in the grocery store has had such significant increases in cost, frozen turkey, steak, dried beans, potatoes, pasta and flour have also significantly outpaced inflation over the last twenty years.

Many people struggle to gauge grocery prices because companies can hide them by changing the quality, weight and packaging of their product. According to consumerist.com, in 2014, Frito-Lay reduced the size of their sun chip bags from 10 oz. to only 7 oz.[5] This removed about a third of the chips in every bag, but the price remained the same. Some companies chose to keep bags of their products the same size and just add additional air to make consumers think that they are still getting the same deal as they did before portions were reduced.

The increase in grocery prices might be explained by greater gas taxes or environmental laws. These result in increased overhead costs and make it more expensive to grow and transport food. Higher prices for food could also be due to changes in government subsidies for crops in which the government essentially pays farmers to buy their food and keep it off the market to manage prices. However, food prices are hardly as concerning as many other goods and services that will be covered in this chapter.

One metric that has greatly outpaced inflation is transit. Toll roads, parking costs, individual driving costs, and public transit systems such as subways are part of this category. Most transit costs tend to be an especially large expense for people living in densely populated areas of the United States such as Chicago, San Francisco, Los Angeles, Boston, and New York City. These costs go widely unnoticed to those who are in a position to afford them, but can add up quickly and be a huge challenge for the millions that commute to save money on rent.

I grew up in San Francisco, and noticed how every year toll roads became more expensive. It was surprising how much it cost to cross a bridge every day. For many years, people worked in toll booths featured on multiple bay area bridges, but several years ago these people were replaced by a new technology called the FasTrak. The FasTrak is a small electronic device placed on the commuter's windshield to track their tolls. The government also introduced a system that tracks license plates and sends the toll bills to residents' addresses. You would expect that this process is more efficient so there would be a decrease in toll prices.

One of the most memorable toll bridges from my childhood was the Golden Gate Bridge. There is a one-way southbound toll on this bridge which has existed since 1937. On January 1st, 1989, the Golden Gate Bridge introduced a $20 ticket book for sixteen trips across the toll bridge which came out to be $1.25/trip. If you did not have a ticket book, it would cost $2 for a car, and for autos with a trailer the toll was $3.[6] As of 2019, one trip across the Golden Gate Bridge would cost you $8.35 or $7.35 if you had a FasTrak. An auto with a one-axle trailer would cost you $22.05 and a two-axle trailer would cost $29.40. People who drove a car in 2019 without a FasTrak paid almost twice as much proportionally for a trip across the same bridge as they did in 1989. People who drove an auto with a two-axle trailer spent almost five times as much as they did in 1989.

I recently took a trip to a writers conference in Los Angeles and was charged $7.76 to access a one-way toll road. When toll roads were introduced, they acted as a fund to help recoup the cost of road construction and maintenance. However, as the population has continued to rise in major cities, the government has raised rates in an effort to incentivize people to drive less, and use more carpools in the hope of combating traffic at a profit. At what point are toll roads considered excessive or price gauging? In places like the Interstate 66 in northern Virginia the government established express lanes that act as uncapped toll roads with prices based on traffic congestion. The Washington Post has reported that this toll highway has hit as high $40 for a one-time use.[7] How are workers expected to thrive if they have to pay an extra $200 in a single week for a toll road? How are young people supposed to get anywhere paying these outrageous government fees?

In addition to higher toll road prices, there are also more toll roads than there were just twenty years ago. Places like northern California have toll roads every few miles. According to the United States Department of Transportation, in 1995 there were approximately 7000 kilometers of toll roads, and in 2015, there were nearly 10,000 kilometers.[8] [9] This is almost a 50% increase in the amount of toll roads in the past twenty years.

People who live in more populous areas are also finding themselves paying increasingly more for the use of a subway. On January 1, 1990, the subway fare in New York City was raised from $1 to $1.15. In 2017, the price of a SingleRide ticket was $3.[10] The cost of using the subway for a SingleRide ticket in 2017 was 35% more expensive than it was in 1990 when adjusting for inflation.

Another major issue with transit is the increasing cost of parking. According to the Seattle Times, the price to park at a 2-hour meter in central Seattle in 1990 was $1 per hour. In 2011, the price increased to $4 an hour.[11] Today's rates are twice as expensive per hour compared to the rates in 1990 when adjusted for inflation. A study by CBS shows that parking costs in Los Angeles amount to more than $3.7 billion a year, and that the average driver spends 85 hours per year searching for parking, at a cost of $1,785 per driver in wasted time, fuel and emissions.[12] It is important to realize just how much higher these transit costs are today compared to just a few years ago.

Individual driving costs have also seen a relatively significant jump when compared to inflation. Since 1950, the American Automobile Association (AAA) has released an annual report called "Your Driving Costs." This report analyzes the costs of owning and operating a new vehicle in the United States. In 2016, the techniques used for obtaining the report information were altered, so the 1995 and 2015 reports are used as references since they contain the same methodology. Operating Costs in these reports are broken down into three categories: gasoline and oil, maintenance, and tires. They are then displayed on a cost per mile average. The 1995 report showed these three values as 5.8¢, 2.6¢ and 1.2¢ respectively, for a total cost of 9.6¢ a mile.[13]

The 2015 report showed these values as 11.2¢, 5.11¢ and .98¢ respectively, for a total cost of 17.3¢ a mile.[14] When adjusted for inflation, both *gasoline and oil* and *maintenance* were approximately 25% more expensive in 2015 than they were in 1995. Interestingly enough, tires are about half as expensive, as they now last significantly longer than they did 20–25 years ago.

While the costs of transit are of concern, they are hardly as important as the continuing rise in the prices of tuition for higher education. The CollegeBoard reported that in 1987, the average private universities had a cost of $15,160 per year, while the average public four-year had a cost of $3,190 per year (these numbers are in inflation-adjusted 2017 dollars). Furthermore, CollegeBoard also reported that in 1997, the average private universities had a cost of $21,020 per year, while the average public four-year had a cost of $4,740 per year. In 2017, the average private university cost $34,740 per year, and the average public university cost $9,970 per year.[15]

According to CollegeBoards numbers, today's students are paying more than three times the tuition costs for public four-year colleges compared to what people paid in 1987. Since 1997, prices of higher education are proportionately 66% higher for private universities and more than twice as expensive for public four-year universities. Clearly stated, the cost for public universities has tripled in the last thirty years and doubled in the last twenty. At what point does going to college become a poor investment of time, energy and money?

The cost of higher education is one of the biggest issues facing younger generations in America. Unfortunately, this growing problem is getting little publicity and is being largely ignored by the media. Why is the pursuit of knowledge and aiming to get a better job becoming so unaffordable? The next several chapters will attempt to tackle our county's education crisis.

Transit costs and higher education have both significantly outpaced inflation in recent years, but there are still many other services and industries that are more expensive than they were for the previous generations. One of these industries is Health Care. From 1999 to 2009 monthly spending increases occurred in families' health insurance premiums (from $490 to $1,115), out-of-pocket health spending rose (from $135 to $235), and taxes devoted to health care rose (from $345 to $440). This is up 131% in a time period in which inflation rose only 28%.[16] Furthermore, health care costs in the United States are the most expensive of any country in the world, but what is causing this? Unlike many other industries, there are many plausible reasons for our extremely high health care costs.

One of the culprits for increases in health care costs is our shifting population dynamics. The second largest generation (the baby boomers) are soon hitting their 70s and there are more elderly people in the United States than any other time in history. This is creating an increased demand for medical care and the younger generations are paying higher rates to supplement the older generation. This will be talked about in greater detail in a later chapter of this book.

Another cause of high medical costs is U.S. tort laws (malpractice lawsuits). In 2013, an article in the Journal of Patient Safety estimated that between 210,000 to 400,000 people die every year in the U.S. from hospital medical errors.[17] In addition, a 2011 study in the New England Journal of Medicine found that roughly 7% or 1 in 14 U.S. doctors face a malpractice suit every year.[18] Many of these lawsuits can be exorbitantly expensive and result in increased cost for medical care. One such case occurred in 2014, where the City of New York and EMS were directed to pay a $172 million dollar settlement to a 12-year-old girl named Tiffany Apple-white. The ambulance that arrived in response to her 911 call was not equipped with advanced life support equipment and delays in transporting her to the hospital left Tiffany paralyzed with severe brain damage. In this case a jury awarded compensation for past and future pain, suffering, loss of enjoyment and medical expenses.[19] It's not surprising to see why medical care is so expensive when the slightest mistake may result in a multimillion dollar lawsuit.

While population dynamics and lawsuits may be somewhat responsible for increasing medical costs, perhaps the largest cause is the price of pharmaceutical drugs. Like medical costs, pharmaceutical drugs have also outpaced inflation significantly in recent years. According to MIT, since 1995, a group of 58 leading cancer drugs has increased in price by 10% annually, even when adjusted for inflation and incremental health benefits. In 1995, cancer drugs in this group cost about $54,100 for each year of life they were estimated to add; by 2013, such drugs cost about $207,000 for each additional year of life.[20] These cancer drugs are roughly 250% more expensive than they were in 1995 when adjusted for inflation. Are these constant price increases reasonable?

The United States has the highest drug use and highest drug prices of any country in the world. According to Jeff Hays' documentary film, *Doctored*, the U.S. accounts for only 5% of the world population, yet consumes 50% of Big Pharmaceutical company drugs.[21] Perhaps even more interesting is the fact that the exact same name brand drugs that other countries use are in many cases sold for significantly higher prices in the U.S. than any other country. A 2015 comparative price report conducted by The International Federation of Health Plans showed seven popular pharmaceutical drug costs compared in Spain, Switzerland, South Africa, The United States and the United Kingdom. The study found that six of the seven drugs had the highest prices in the United States. One example was the drug Humira (prescribed to treat rheumatoid arthritis). In 2015, this drug cost $552 in South Africa, $822 in Switzerland, $1,253 in Spain, $1,362 in the United Kingdom and

$2,669 in the United States.[22] Why are the costs of drugs so high in the U.S.? Why are U.S. customers paying five times more for the same drug than the price that people pay in South Africa? One reason may be the amount of money Big Pharma spends on congressional lobbyists. In just the first quarter of 2016, thirty-eight major drugmakers and trade groups spent more than $50 million, according to Kaiser Health News analysis.[23]

Interestingly enough, The United States and New Zealand are the only two countries where direct-to-consumer (DTC) advertising of prescription drugs is legal. Unfortunately, in today's society medical professionals and psychiatrists rely heavily on prescription drugs as a primary source of treatment, rather than trying to help patients in other ways.

While health care and astronomical drug prices are hurting young Americans, perhaps even greater damage is coming from rent prices. According to the U.S. Census the median rent in the United States in the year 2000, was more than twice as high (inflation adjusted) as rent in 1950. Rent in places like California, New Jersey and Florida were found to be nearly three times as high (inflation adjusted) during the same time period.[24] Although sources tend to disagree on the exact amount, many claim previous generations that grew up in the 50s and 60s spent only 20–30% of their income on rent while today people are spending 40–50% of their income and in some areas even higher. This is especially damaging to young people who make lower wages than their elders due to being in the early stages of their career. According to RENTcafé, a popular rent comparison tool, in February 2020, the average one-bedroom apartment in San Francisco cost $3,629 per month.[25] This goes to further demonstrate how in today's society, rent can be viewed as very constraining towards the progression of people in general. Progressive taxes further exasperate the problem. Are we moving toward a society where only the rich will be able to afford renting or owning a property?

While folks are finding themselves paying increasingly higher rents, they are also seeing the rising costs of utilities. The cost of electricity has surged in some areas due to the rise of regulations and a lack of competition, but water is a significantly bigger concern. According to the U.S. department of energy, between 1993 and 2007 water prices based on U.S. Region have increased 95% on the west coast and 74% in the south west.[26] Droughts as well as water infrastructure deterioration are cited as being the main causes for this increase.

Another factor that contributes to increasing water prices is the depletion of aquifers (ground water) across the country. As populations continue to grow and water continues to deplete, prices will continue to rise. Increasing rent and utilities can be especially harmful to young Americans because they are considered necessities, so owners of these services can get away with overcharging because few people would refuse to buy the service. Will there ever be a point where people refuse to rent places because they are too expensive? When will increasing water prices cause people to stop buying government water and resort to rainwater? Only time will tell.

The last industry covered in this chapter is the entertainment industry. It is yet another example of a service that has outpaced inflation. Although entertainment is considered to be a bit of a luxury service, this is unfortunate as many younger parents are finding it impossible to take their kids to the type of events that they were able to attend when they were a child. One such place that has seen a large increase in prices is Disneyland.

In January 2004, a Disneyland Southern California Select Annual Pass cost $99 and a Disneyland Resort Southern California Annual Pass cost $129. In February 2018, these two different passes cost $369 and $499 respectively.[27] Both of these passes are more than two and a half times as expensive as they were just 16 years ago. Has Disneyland really added so much that they can justify such a radical price increase? Some argue that these increases in Disneyland prices were used to combat overcrowding that made ride lines longer, but should young children miss out on this experience just because of how much it costs?

Other examples of price increases in the entertainment industry are cable prices and NFL ticket prices. According to the FCC, the average price for expanded basic cable service was $22.35 in July, 1995. As of January 2015, the average price had increased to $69.03.[28] The price for cable was more than twice as expensive inflation-adjusted in 2015 as it was in 1995. More channels have been added, but is this cost increase justified, or is it just greed?

NFL tickets have also seen a substantial increase, and this is omitting the increased stadium parking costs. According to Statista, the National Football League average ticket price increased from $62.38 in 2006 to $92.98 in 2016.[29] Ticket prices in 2016 cost 20% more than just 10 years earlier. While in the past, many young people went to games together, these increases are making it harder to do so.

The main point of this chapter is to get people to realize just how much less purchasing power young people have in today's economy in comparison to past generations. This chapter just represents a few of the most extreme cases where the cost of a good or service has greatly outpaced inflation. There are still many more examples where things are significantly more expansive than they used to be.

Why are wages staying relatively stagnant when so many costs are increasing at such a rapid rate? To make matters worse, why are we constantly paying more for taxes? At what point do goods and services become so expensive that people can no longer afford them? Imagine how much money your first job paid. Perhaps you made $4, $5 or even $10 an hour. Would you have been willing to work the job for $3 an hour? What about $2 an hour? At what point would you have no longer been motivated to have a job because wages were too low in proportion to costs? This is the motivational challenge that many young people are facing in America today. But despite all the challenges coming from higher costs, perhaps a bigger concern is debt.

CHAPTER 3

The History and Consequences of Debt

Americans are addicted to debt. We use it to buy houses, go to college, purchase cars, found businesses and buy other day-to-day needs with a piece of plastic called a credit card. Our society has evolved to live outside of their means, failing to realize just how much debt impacts their lives. Newer generations are facing a higher debt burden than any generations that preceded them.

According to the Federal Reserve Bank of New York, household debt increased in the first quarter of 2018, for the 15th consecutive quarter, to become $536 billion higher than the previous peak of $12.68 trillion in 2008. In the United States there are four main sources which make up approximately 94% of the $13.21 trillion of household debt. Currently mortgages make up about 68%, college loans make up 11%, auto loans account for 9% and credit card debt accounts for 6%.[30]

What events brought us to this point? How did debt evolve into something that controls so many people and has become such a major part of people's overhead? Most people believe that debt, loans and consumer credit are relatively new concepts, but these practices have in fact been around for thousands of years.

It is said that the origination of consumer credit started over 5,000 years ago in Sumer, an ancient city located in what is modern-day

Iraq. The first written account of consumer credit took place in 1800 BC, when the city of Babylon established formal written laws that would become known as the Code of Hammurabi. These laws set appropriate punishments for crimes and wages, but also established the maximum interest rates that could be used on things like grain and silver.

Other societies also incorporated debt into their culture and created new structures of debt. Ancient Greece and Rome were the first to establish pawnbrokers which allowed lending with items used as collateral. This would offer more protection for lenders and many pawnshops still exist in modern society. In the early 1600s, indentured servants first arrived in America, and for several hundred years this was a popular debt instrument in which poor people would work off their debt by laboring on a lender's property. My grandfather was one of these people, and came to America with no money and paid off his trip by working as an indentured servant. However, despite the thousands of years of debt and credit practices across dozens of cultures, most of the laws and practices that define our modern society came out of the great depression.

In the early 1900s, people would typically put 50% down on a house and then take out a mortgage that lasted only three to five years. Unlike today's mortgages, you paid only the interest each month and then a huge lump sum at the end of your mortgage period. In the case of a $1,000 dollar house and three-year mortgage you would put $500 down, pay the interest every month until the three-year mark, and then you would pay off the other $500. However, this system was short-lived and one of many to be changed after the great depression.

In 1934, FDR established The Federal Housing Administration (FHA). The FHA was built to restore confidence in lenders and reduce their risk by lowering the probability of default. The FHA created quality standards, lowered down-payment requirements, created the 15- and 30-year mortgage and introduced the concept of amortization periods where people would pay off loan principle and interest at the same time. This new creation helped strengthen lending and seemed to work wonderfully. According to the census of housing, homeownership rates would rise from 43.6% in 1940 to 61.9% in 1960.[31] That's almost 20% in only 20 years. Many history books and professors praise FDR's creation of the FHA as a great idea that helped America, and it's not surprising that they would think that way, but the introduction of the FHA created incentives that led to a lot of high risks in today's mortgage and financial industry.

People respond to incentives. In modern times, the incentive given to banks is to give out as many loans as possible. Simply spoken, more loans equate to more profits. To put even more fuel on the fire, mortgage loan officers who work for these banks typically get paid 1% commission of the total loan amount that they give out. Since these people rely on commission, it is in their best interest to give out as many loans as possible, even when it is to people who cannot afford them. This has created a system where banks can act recklessly and give out many bad loans. It also caused banks to create new types of mortgages to build an even larger demand.

One new type of mortgage that was introduced was the Adjustable rate mortgage (ARM). ARMs were a product of the 1980s. Unlike traditional fixed-rate mortgages which featured the same interest rate throughout a loan term, ARMs have interest rates that fluctuate over the course of a mortgage. This allows people with lower incomes to have access to buying a home. ARMs often feature extremely low introductory interest rates, but if those rates rise, many people will be unable to make the minimum payments and will lose their houses like they did during the 2008 housing crisis. As prices in houses have continued to skyrocket and there are more obvious red flags, the banks are still more eager than ever to give out mortgages. Many are pushing for larger and larger mortgages to "help" people afford houses. In recent years, banks introduced jumbo mortgages which are massive loan amounts above conventional loan limits. In today's market, banks are literally immune to all negative financial consequences of their behavior. Since banks will be the first to be bailed out in a financial crisis why wouldn't they introduce the most outlandish mortgages possible?

What most people fail to realize is that the creation of FHA and modern banking standards helped to create more artificial demand for houses using debt. In the short term, during the 1950s and 1960s, easy-to-get mortgages helped more people own houses, but as demand became higher, prices also became higher. This system created something that I call "Mortgage Wars," where invisible money and mortgages have inflated housing prices to ridiculous levels.

According to the census of housing, in 1940, the median home value in the U.S. was $2,938. By 1980, the price had risen to $47,200, and by 2000, it had risen to $119,600. Even adjusted for inflation, the median home price in 1940 would only have been $30,600 in 2000 dollars.[32] Based on this information it can be concluded that millennials are paying (or should I say taking loans out for) almost four times more for a house in comparison to their grandparents. Mortgages are in fact a massive ponzi scheme where each generation is paying more money and forced to borrow more to buy a house. In today's society most people are not bidding on a house to own with cash, they are borrowing money and having their mortgage fight with other prospective bidder's mortgages. However, interest rates, wages, and the illusion of inflation have acted as a clever way to disguise this. A great example is home prices from 1990 to 2015.

According to the average and median amounts of net compensation chart provided by the Social Security Administration, the median income in America in 1990, was $14,498.74 or approximately $14,500 a year. In 2015, the median income was $29,930.13 or approximately $30,000 a year.[33] The Federal Reserve Bank of St. Louis reports that in 1990, the average interest rate was approximately 10%, and in 2015 it was 3.9%.[34] Furthermore, the median housing price for a new home in 1990 was approximately $120,000 and in 2015, the median housing price for a new home was approximately $300,000.[35]

A $120,000, 30-year mortgage at 10% interest, would amount to a payment of approximately $1,053 a month. In 1990, someone would spend $12,636 (of their $14,500) assuming they had a median income job. This equates to spending 87% of their income on their mortgage during this time period. A $300,000, 30-year mortgage at 3.9% interest, would amount to a payment of $1,415 a month. In 2015, someone would spend $16,980 (of their $30,000) or about 57% of their income on their mortgage, assuming they had a median income job during this time period. This means that in 2015 people were paying roughly 30% less per year from their take-home for a mortgage than in 1990. This makes everything appear to be fine; after all, houses are so much cheaper. But the real issue is all the invisible money propping up the system.

What most consumers fail to understand is just how much of their money is going toward interest. Now suppose someone has a $250,000 mortgage. If they decide to get a 10-year mortgage and assume a 3.75% interest rate, they will pay $300,183.73 total on that $250,000. This amounts to over $50,000 paid in interest. On a 20-year mortgage one would pay $355,732.99 which equates to about $105,000 in interest. On a 30-year mortgage one would pay $416,804.03 of which about $165,000 is interest. Simply put, the longer the span of the mortgage the more interest.

A big challenge many people of newer generations face is that it is nearly impossible for the average single earner to afford anything except a 30-year or longer mortgage. Essentially you have the illusion of choice when the choice has already been made for you. For example, a 10-year, $250,000 mortgage at 3.75% interest would require a monthly payment of $2,501.53 which is mathematically impossible for a median income earner to afford because the cost is higher than their $2100 monthly income. A 20-year mortgage of the same size and interest would require a monthly payment of $1,482.22 which is quite difficult and probably not doable for most median income earners because the cost of their mortgage and basic living expenses will be higher than the wage they make. A 30-year $250,000 mortgage at 3.75% interest would require a monthly payment of $1,157.79 which is possible and grants about $900 a month in spending money for food, utilities, and other basic expenses. This will make every month financially very tight. When people can no longer afford 30-year mortgages does everyone move to 40-year mortgages or 50-year mortgages to satisfy the banks' need to write never-ending amounts of loans?

According to the Board of Governors of the Federal Reserve System, during the first quarter of 1990, mortgage debt outstanding for all holders was $3.63 trillion. Adjusted to 2015 numbers this was approximately $6.78 trillion. In 2015, during the first quarter, mortgage debt outstanding for all holders had risen to $13.5 trillion.[36] Proportionately speaking, there is more than twice as much outstanding mortgage debt in the United States in the last 25 years.

Although financing companies may have reduced the amount of subprime and deep subprime loans that were fabled to have led to the 2008 market collapse, nothing is stopping them from creating special new loan programs where borrowers are able to obtain a mortgage with absurdly low down-payments. According to the Realtors Confidence Index, for all buyers whose transaction closed in February 2017, 62% of those who obtained a mortgage made a down payment of less than 20%. Among first-time homebuyers, 65% of buyers put down 0 to 6%.[37] This is disturbing because when the real estate market crashes, many people will be left upside down on their mortgage. This means that those who took out financing would owe more on their house than it was worth. Since buyers are putting lower down payments on houses, when a crash hits, these buyers could just walk away from their house, causing a massive economic downturn in real estate similar to that in 2007.

It would be painful for people to leave their house as well as difficult to reestablish credit, but why would someone have a $500,000 loan on a house that is worth $200,000? The question is how much longer will it take for our current mortgage system to fall apart? How many more generations will be robbed of their future by excessive bank loans? Will millennials enjoy the same type of home appreciation and massive profits as their baby boomer counterparts? It is highly unlikely.

In ten years the youngest baby boomers will reach 79 years old, the average age of death in the United States. As these people die off, who will be buying the real estate they leave behind? It's unlikely that today's millennials who are more in debt than any other generation before them will ever be able to afford buying a house with these crazy real estate prices. Future real estate market stability will be largely dependent on an influx of wealthy immigrants into the country.

Although mortgages are the biggest source of household debt in the United States, college loans are becoming an increasingly larger problem. While college loans do not get nearly as much press coverage as mortgages, millions of millennials are struggling to pay off these loans and newer graduates are facing larger loans every year. Recently, student loan debt overtook credit card debt. There is more than $1.3 trillion of student loan debt in the United States. In comparison to other countries, a higher education in the United States is one of the least affordable in the world.

According to the Proceedings from a National Symposium on December 10, 1997, the average student loan debt in 1996 was $11,950 for public four-year bachelor's degrees.[38] Fox News reports that the average class of 2016 graduate had a whopping $37,172 in student loan debt.[39] Adjusting for inflation from 1996 to 2016, $11,950 would have the same purchasing power as $18,336.44. This math shows that today's young people have proportionately at least twice as much college debt as the graduates from twenty years ago when adjusted for inflation. This is hardly surprising though, considering how much college tuition prices have outpaced inflation. But what is causing this ridiculous increase in price and debt? There are two main culprits.

One cause of rising college debt is government intervention. This is occurring through both programs and loans. In 1944, the government passed an important piece of legislation called the Servicemen's Readjustment Act which is better known as the GI Bill. This bill was originally introduced to provide benefits for returning WWII Veterans. Some of the benefits included were low-cost mortgages and payments for tuition to attend a university, high school or other form of education. This bill helped millions of people in the armed forces and incentivized them to grab new skills for free or at a lower cost, but it also created a higher demand for college in the process, which pushed up prices. In 2010, the government passed the Montgomery & Post 9/11 GI Bill. These bills expanded eligibility to include members of the National Guard, created Spousal GI Bill eligibility, and changed the tuition cap. This helped to create an even larger college demand.

It has also been found in recent years that many for-profit institutions that accept the GI bill have engaged in predatory lending and have acted in ways that have misled and deceived veterans. One article suggests that at eight of the ten for-profits that take in the most GI Bill cash, more than half of students drop out within a year of matriculation.[40] In fact, the issue of predatory colleges has become so prevalent that in 2012, President Barack Obama signed Executive Order 13607 to try and combat this problem.

Another way the government gets involved in higher education is through student loans. This includes Stafford, Parent PLUS and Perkins loans. Stafford loans are the most common and feature two variations, unsubsidized and subsidized. Currently, Subsidized Federal Stafford Loans have an interest rate of 6.8% and Direct Unsubsidized Loans have an interest rate of 4.29%. These loans can be very large, and graduate students have a lifetime aggregate loan limit of $138,500. This loan is about the same size as what the previous generation held in mortgage loans.

The big problem with Stafford loans is that they are extremely easy to obtain and almost no one can be denied even if they have low earnings or bad credit. The idea of giving people loans so that everyone can afford to go to college has led to increased demand for higher education. This increased demand has allowed higher education institutions to raise tuition rates and these rate increases affect people from all social classes, not just the poor. This of course gives birth to several questions. At what point have college loans gone too far, and at what point is it no longer worth it to attend college?

In today's market, a student with an average amount of debt, a Subsidized Federal Stafford Loan at 6.8%, and a 10-year payment plan, will have a payment of approximately $428 per month. If a student has a 4.29% interest rate, their payment would be $392 per month. Either way, your average college loan will cost about $400 per month. This means that $2.50 will go towards a loan for every hour worked in a forty-hour work week. A college grad with an average sized loan making less than $12.50 an hour is making effectively less than minimum wage ($10 an hour minimum wage). Keep in mind that the median wage in America is only $14.42 an hour or $30k per year as discussed earlier in this chapter.

The second big contributor to the massive increase in the size of college loans occurred when congress passed the Bankruptcy Abuse Prevention and Consumer Protection Act of 2005. This law makes all college debt guaranteed by Sallie Mae and makes college debt nondischargeable in bankruptcy. Because all private loans are guaranteed, debt companies are effectively motived to lend out as much as possible, even to people who cannot afford the repayments. Loan companies have zero responsibility for their actions. If this poorly constructed law was removed, lenders might be more careful about whom they lend to and how much, and the cost of higher education would eventually go down.

The last major source of debt to be covered in this chapter is auto debt. According to the Federal Reserve Bank of St. Louis, the U.S. closed out 2016 with just shy of $1.1 trillion in outstanding auto loan debt. This is about 3.8 times the debt of 1990 when it was roughly $290 billion.[41] Adjusted for inflation, these 1990 numbers would equate to $562 billion or about half of the auto debt that we have today. Car loans are becoming a larger burden on Americans every year. According to Experian the average payment for a new car was $483 a month in 2015, and used car loans averaged $361 a month during the same time period.[42] A study by GOBankingRates claims that the average cost of a new car has risen from $19,085.19 in 1990 (adjusted for inflation) to $35,263 in 2018.[43] Although auto loans and car prices are higher today than in 1990, they are not the only reason why there is so much more consumer auto debt.

One reason people have more auto debt relates to how the government responded to the 2007 financial crisis. This crisis and the 2003–2008 energy crisis, combined with extreme greed, poor business practices and bad management caused General Motors and Chrysler, to file for Chapter 11 bankruptcies in mid-2009. The automotive industry was hammered as gas prices hit record highs and the purchases of high profit gas guzzler SUVs and pickup trucks fell to record lows. Congress responded by granting a $25 billion loan to the auto industry and President Bush agreed to an emergency bailout of $17.4 billion. Despite these efforts to save the industry, the auto market still looked shaky at best. The government then proceeded to pass the "Cash for Clunkers" program to stimulate consumer spending. This government program gave the incentive to trade in old run-down vehicles for newer cars with better gas efficiency. This may have helped to save the automotive industry, but at the same time, it promoted more automotive debt as everyone rushed to get newer cars.

Most financial professionals argue that one of the main causes of the 2007–2008 economic collapse in the housing market was higher risk loans. These high risk loans are often referred to as subprime, and deep subprime. A subprime loan is a loan given to someone who has a credit score between 501 and 600, and a deep subprime loan is a loan given to someone who has a credit score between 300 and 500. While banks have stopped giving out as many loans to these high-risk individuals for real estate, the auto industry has continued to give out these dangerous loans in droves. According to Experian Information solutions 2015 statistics, subprime loans make up 28% and deep subprime loans make up about 6% of used auto loans.[42*] This means that more than a third of all the loans on used cars are either subprime or deep subprime and have very high risk. The worst culprits of these high risk loans are finance institutions and car dealers. Car dealers have a special term for their loans. It's called Buy Here Pay Here (BHPH). One of the reasons for this increase in bad loans is an oversupply of used cars. Interestingly enough, this is being caused by a huge influx of millennials, who are leasing cars and giving them back, rather than buying them. Unfortunately, many of these young people don't understand why leasing cars is such a poor financial decision.

According to Edmunds.com from Q2 of 2011 to Q2 of 2016 the number of car leases grew from 1.1 million to 2.2 million. Millennials and people over the age of 75 are the two generations that lease the most cars, and a higher percentage of women lease than men. Some of the vehicles with the biggest increases in leasing since 2011 are Land Rover (134%), Volkswagen (131%), GMC (112%), Kia (103%) and Chevrolet (94%), but most leasing is still primarily for luxury and premium cars.[44] On average, monthly lease payments are 23% lower than the monthly purchase payments. However, this might not be so good for the economy in the long run. In leasing there is no disclosure on cost of capital or interest because it is technically not a loan. Most auto companies charge you about 14% in interest for leasing a car.

There are vast numbers of people leasing cars they can't afford. Who wouldn't want to show off in a new Lamborghini? The problem is that a leased car can no longer be considered an asset, but rather a cost. The fact that most people only lease cars for two or three years and then trade them in for newer vehicles means that they will never own a car. While the older generation paid off loans that would eventually disappear, many young people have fallen into the trap of car lease payments that never end.

This chapter aims to educate people on the history of debt and how things got to where they are today. As you can see, debt has become a major problem, but has also woven itself deep into American culture. Unfortunately, newer generations are finding themselves with a much larger debt burden than people from previous generations, but where does all of this stop? Can it be that people have simply forgotten how to live within their means, or have we lost the ability to comprehend a budget? In Ecclesiastes 8:9, a wise man wrote that "man has dominated man to his injury." Perhaps the systems that we have built to govern our economy will also be the ones that could have the greatest negative impacts on our lives. Debt is a big issue, but so are the changes in overhead and spending that it creates. Is this debt and increasing cost of living leading to a lower standard of living for newer generations?

CHAPTER 4

The Battle for an Unsustainable Lifestyle

Standard of living can be defined as the degree of wealth and material comfort available to a person or community. Many economists support the idea that as we increase economic production, we also increase our standard of living. The idea is that if we produce more, we can consume more. The argument commonly used to support this can be illustrated by the fact that the average people of newer generations have access to things like cell phones and TVs when thirty to forty years ago these goods were considered luxury items only obtainable by the rich. It is suggested that advances in technology, production and efficiency, combined with greater competition have brought the prices of these items down to where nearly anyone can afford them. This of course results in an upsurge of consumption. However, since 1973 there has been a significant divergence between pay and productivity. Today's working class Americans are producing far more, but this has not resulted in proportional increases in wages. According to the Economic Policy Institute,

"From 1973 to 2017, net productivity rose 77.0 percent, while the hourly pay of typical workers essentially stagnated— increasing only 12.4 percent over 44 years (after adjusting for inflation). This means that although Americans are working more productively than ever, the fruits of their labors have primarily accrued to those at the top and to corporate profits, especially in recent years."[45]

While newer generations may have access to groundbreaking technological innovations and increases in economic production, they are also paying proportionately more for many goods and services and are struggling with increasing amounts of debt as covered in the last two chapters. In many cases these younger people are enjoying increased consumption, but at a price. This chapter focuses on how the concepts covered in the last two chapters are affecting the lives of the younger generations and aims to ask the question: how can we measure generational progress?

Poverty has long stood as one of the major metrics to determine the health of America. Many people believe that fewer poor people equates to a better country. Although there has always been poverty, today's poverty has been cleverly disguised and hidden by debt. Even those who appear to be doing well and have nice furniture, pretty wall hangings and an extravagant kitchen are often drowning in debt.

According to Jillian Berman, a reporter at MarketWatch, in 1989, the net worth of all 25 to 34 year olds, regardless of whether they had student loans was $25,786 when adjusted to 2016 dollars, however as of 2016 this same age bracket has seen their median net worth fall to just $12,000.[46] This shows that the net worth of today's young people between 25 and 34 is less than half of what it was for the previous generation. However, even though this is an important statistic to notice, perhaps a better marker of generational progress is your average person's overhead.

A person's true financial health is not determined by the amount of money they make every month; it is determined by what they can save each month. A big part of what drives savings is overhead.

When I say overhead, I am referring to one's monthly expenses, namely the expenses that they can't live without. Some costs are food, water, rent/mortgages, car payments, cell phone, insurances, student loans, and credit cards. How much is someone really able to save each month after all their bills are paid? As mentioned in the last chapter the median wage for an individual in America is only roughly $14.42 per hour, which equates to a gross pay of $30,000 a year and roughly $25,000 after taxes. This is about $2,100 dollars a month. But what can you afford with only $2,100 a month? Money may not be able to buy you happiness, but it can make problems go away that make you unhappy.

Using the numbers from the previous chapters, a person will pay roughly $800 a month on median rent (on the bottom end), have an average student loan payment of $400 a month, and have a used car loan costing about $360 a month. Just these three expenses add up to $1,560 a month or about 75% of the median net paycheck. This isn't even including the costs of food, gas, utilities, and insurances. The point of this is to show just how tight living expenses are for your average individual living in today's society.

Ben Shapiro, a popular republican conservative once said:
"The reason people are permanently poor in the United States is not because they don't have money, it's because they suck with money. The reason why people are temporarily poor is because they don't have money."[47]

Ben may have been right if he used baby boomers as an example, but there is sufficient evidence to conclude that many members of the newer generations can be permanently poor despite their best efforts. In contrast to previous generations, a vast majority of young people are living paycheck to paycheck and caught in a vortex because of it. In fact, according to a 2017 study by careerbuilder.com, 78% of people employed full-time in America live paycheck to paycheck.[48]

This is a huge problem because it creates a cycle of stagnation where progress is limited unless an individual's overhead goes down or their pay goes up, thus creating people who are permanently poor.

The increasing financial stress experienced by newer generations has caused some millennials to get regular side hustles or odd jobs. A study by Bankrate concluded that 38% of people from ages 18 to 37 make money from their side hustles at least once a month.[49] Some of the most popular side hustles for millennials are home repair/landscaping, selling or reselling goods online and babysitting. When I graduated college, I began buying items at garage sales, swap meets and estate sales to sell them for profit on ebay. This resulted in several hundred extra dollars a month and helped a lot.

Unfortunately, sometimes even working extra on the side still isn't enough. Many individuals have turned to working longer hours to offset the increased costs of goods and services. According to the Gallup, adults employed full time in the U.S. now work an average of 47 hours per week, with 9% of hourly workers exceeding 60 hours.[50] Furthermore, the Economic Policy Institute reports that the average work year rose from 1,687 hours in 1979 to 1,868 hours in 2007 which represents an increase of 10.7%—the equivalent of every worker working 4.5 additional weeks per year.[51] Despite the extra effort, members of newer generations are still struggling to set money aside for things like investments and retirement plans. Unfortunately, retiring has become a concept that seems outlandish and impossible to many members of the newer generations. This has led many millennials to dismiss it as something that can never happen for them.

In fact, this problem has become so bad that Timberland released a new advertisement targeting millennials that is being displayed at malls in Hong Kong. The ad reads "You're never going to be able to retire. Why should your boots?"[52] Statisticbrain reports that out of

100 people who start working at the age of 25 today, only 4% will have adequate capital stowed away for retirement at the age of 65. They also determined that 63% will be dependent on Social Security, friends, relatives or charity and that 29% will be dead.[53]

The emergence of COVID-19 is adding another challenge to the mix. While COVID-19 is currently affecting everyone, it does seem to have a larger financial impact on millennials. This is because millennials now make up the majority of the workforce and most struggled to gain footing during the 2007–2008 crash. Millions of jobs are currently being lost and most millennials haven't had time to reach peak earning as they are earlier in their careers. Baby boomers may be more likely to get sick, but many are retired and collecting social security. Those that are still working have had a much longer time period to build a career and wealth.

Younger generations are facing a much more difficult financial battle than previous generations. This is putting a lot of pressure on young people to cut their costs any way possible to live a higher quality life. They are attempting to do this in several ways.

Not surprisingly, one of the tactics many millennials are using to cut costs is to have fewer children. The government keeps track of new child births in something called the fertility rate. The 2018 birthrate was 59.1 births per 1,000 women. This is the lowest ever recorded since the government started keeping statistics in 1909. The current fertility rate is about half of what it was during its all-time high in 1957. During that time period, the fertility rate was 122.9 births per 1,000 women.[54] This leads to an important question. If everyone is having fewer children, this will lead to a smaller workforce, and if we have a smaller workforce, how do we support all of the older people in retirement?

Another way millennials are slashing costs is by attempting to cut their renting expenses. This is leading young people to have two options, either roommates or multigenerational households. While previous generations typically only had roommates during their teenage years and college experiences, some members of newer generations are finding themselves with roommates for far longer. According to Zillow, 30% of working-age adults—aged 23 to 65— live in doubled-up households, up from a low of 21% in 2005.[55] But how many roommates are too many, and at what point does it defeat the entire purpose of moving out?

In previous chapters, it was briefly mentioned that many younger people are living with their parents longer. Some make this a more permanent arrangement. This is what has come to be known as multigenerational households and is quite common in the Far East. It is considered normal for residents in countries like Japan and China to have two or even three generations living under one roof. This concept has been slowly migrating to America. According to the Pew research center, a record 64 million Americans live in multigenerational households, which is nearly twice as many as the 35.4 million people who lived in multigenerational households in 1990.[56] But this can be challenging on both parents and their older children, primarily due to American culture.

Many parents look forward to their kids moving into their own place. While parents love their children, they can sometimes feel like a bit of a burden. When the kids move out, parents often have the feeling of owning their own lives again and this awards them the feeling of freedom. However, moving out in today's financially constrained economy can be tough from the kids' point of view as well. It's difficult to enjoy one's independence when you spend the vast majority of your paycheck on rent and struggle to save money, that said, not making the leap can often come with harsh judgement. This can be especially difficult for young men who are often pressured to be the breadwinners in society. Many women find a man who still lives with his parents significantly less desirable. In this case the culture in America puts pressure on young people to make a financially bad decision.

One of the biggest challenges for young people lies in the realization that the lifestyles experienced by previous generations are simply no longer obtainable, and that newer generations need to work significantly harder to see the same standard of living as their parents. While some young people have buckled down, put in the extra effort, and made sacrifices, many are experiencing decreased motivation.

To obtain better jobs requires a lot of extra work, commuting and experience. Some question whether they would even want a higher paying job when expectations are typically so much higher, and increased taxes and gas costs for longer commutes largely offset the gains from the pay increase. Furthermore, millennials are dealing with the daunting question of whether they should shell out the money for an education or work more hours to save up for one, when a better job is not guaranteed.

The question is where can millennials go from here. Will they be able to break down the walls that are preventing them from success and rewrite society? Will they be the ones who demand better living conditions and redefine broken systems?

Section I: Five Keys to Success

The first section of this book talked about millennials who are paying more for everyday items and struggle with larger amounts of debt than previous generations. These two underlying issues often lead to stress and can create a decreased standard of living. How might someone address these problems? Here are five ideas that can help people improve their lives and address the challenges discussed in the first four chapters.

1) **Attend Community Meetings and Ask Questions:**
A great way to learn about prices and challenges that small businesses face can come from attending meetings. You may find out about new taxes, laws or challenges that affect price. Most communities have meetings that you can discover by searching for them online. Common meetings include chamber of commerce, board of trade, board of directors, and water board meetings. You can also check your local colleges for speakers, discussions or special guests who act as experts in their field. You can benefit by learning about what is causing cost increases for goods and services and work with other community members to try and solve issues.

2) **Live at Home and Save:**
One of the best bits of advice I received was that life is not a race. If you are a young person and still live with your parents, consider staying a little longer. Work with your parents to help them understand your financial situation and have them read this book. You are not alone in this matter and being able to save extra money to use as a down payment, pay off debt or use in investments, can have a huge positive impact on the rest of your life.

3) **Understand Purchasing Vehicles:**
   You do not need a flashy brand new vehicle. Should you buy one, you lose thousands of dollars the moment you drive it off the lot. You can buy a great used car and save several hundred on your payment every month. Never lease a vehicle you don't intend to buy. This is because you will always have a cost and it will increase your overhead. A vehicle is a means to get from point A to point B and is not a fancy toy. Removing several hundred dollars a month from your overhead can greatly decrease stress and help you save money for things you want to do.

4) **Buy a House You Can Afford:**
   Although I do not suggest buying a house at the top of the market when houses are the most expensive that they have ever been, for some people houses offer a unique level of comfort. If you do plan on buying when real estate prices are high, consider going with a small condo or small house when purchasing your first home and work to move up from there. You should not shoot for a million dollar home for a starter house if you cannot afford it. If you have land, use it for fruit producing trees, gardening or storage. Make your land work for you. Too many people make the mistake of going into too much debt on their house. Saving several hundred a month on a mortgage can lead to a significantly richer life even if your house is a bit smaller.

5) **Minimize Use of a Credit Card:**
   Decide what you want and what you need and try to avoid buying things you just want when using a credit card. It is important to have a small amount of debt and use it to establish credit, but every time you buy something be aware of the high amounts of interest you will pay on that item. Use credit cards sparingly or avoid them when possible. Waiting until you have money to buy something can save you a lot in the long run and make your life a lot easier.

SYSTEMATIC PROBLEMS THAT NEGATIVELY AFFECT THE ECONOMY

CHAPTER 5

The Higher Education Nightmare; What We Can Do to Fix It

Deciding whether or not to attend college has become an extremely important decision for many Americans. However, today's higher education system is difficult to navigate and young people are often misinformed, which can lead them to making bad decisions. There is a lot of pressure on young people who don't want to be singled out for not having a degree when a large portion of their peers have one. At the same time, members of younger generations were told by their parents that education was the key to life, luxury and success, yet in many cases their parents didn't get degrees or had student loans that were drastically lower than the ones taken out by their children.

According to Business Insider, an average 18-year-old in 2017 earned only $17,700 a year.[57] Considering a large portion of incoming college students have worked for minimum wage, or have never had a job, it is difficult for them to understand the repercussions of taking on a $50,000 loan, or what it can potentially buy. A study by One Wisconsin Institute reported that it will take an average of 21.1 years for those graduating in 2013 to pay off their college loans.[58] Does it make sense for someone to spend twenty years paying off the debt they incurred for a four-year bachelor's degree that may or may not result in a quality job?

Another challenge college student's face is a lack of understanding about majors. While all majors tend to cost the same, not all majors result in the same skillsets and future career opportunities. According to a study by Payscale.com, someone majoring in Speech & Drama will earn a median salary of $28,300 with 0–5 years of experience. Meanwhile, someone who aims to receive a degree in Petroleum Engineering is entering a market where the median starting wage is $94,500 with 0–5 years of experience.[59] Most students don't realize that by majoring in low labor demand disciplines like Speech & Drama, they will be more likely to struggle paying off their student loans.

Students can often be misled by universities that exaggerate wages. A recent survey found that 41% of graduates from the classes of 2014 and 2013 earn $25,000 or less per year, while only 15% of the class of 2015 expected to make this amount after graduation.[60] I worked for a temp agency in 2014, and met a man with a master's degree in accounting making only $12 an hour. My first job out of college was an unpaid internship that resulted in a minimum wage job after three months. Quite a few graduates are finding themselves in this depressing situation.

One of the ways colleges distort the reality of wages is through campus-hosted career fairs. This gives students the idea that there are many companies hiring, and after talking to recruiters, young people are led to believe that there is a strong chance they will obtain an entry level job with a high salary. After I graduated, I attended a career fair at my college in which I found out that no one was actually hiring. Why would companies send people to go to a fair when they had no desire to hire anyone? The simple truth is that the universities would benefit by appearing to have connections and thus attract more attention and prospects. Companies benefit from the advertising and analysts who would be led to believe that xyz company was expanding when in fact they weren't hiring. The question to ask is whether companies are actually hiring or just using a career fair as a publicity opportunity.

Another issue young people face is that they go to universities expecting to graduate in four years. The problem is that even though many colleges are called "four-year colleges," students are unlikely to graduate in four years. According to Complete College America, a nonprofit group based in Indianapolis, the number of students that graduate in four years from a four-year institution is only 19%.[61] This is a bad thing for students, but a good thing for most colleges, as they now get to charge you even more money. Why would they try to make college shorter? They want you to be there as long as possible, to maximize profit.

Those who graduate from universities often face another challenge. They often lack experience with specific programs and have no certifications. Desired program knowledge can be easily seen on job boards, yet colleges ignore them. In fields of study such as Business Administration, companies are often looking for experience with programs, such as Salesforce, SAP, Peoplesoft, Excel, Oracle, Adobe and Visio. Employers also like relevant certifications in their field. In project management, there is a high employer demand for certifications from the Project Management Institute such as the PMP. In business, mid- to upper-level managers are searching for someone with certifications in Six Sigma. In IT, many hiring managers look for people that are Certified Information Security Managers (CISM) or Cisco Certified Networking Professionals (CCNP). Shouldn't more certifications be included and integrated into the college curriculum?

There are education sites such as udemy.com and skillshare.com that offer specific classes that tend to deal with programs used in the modern workforce and help people train to obtain certifications. These classes and certifications are all available at a fraction of the cost of a university.

Now when it comes to changing the higher education system, most people tend to fall into one of two groups. People either believe that college should stay tuition based, or people believe it should be free. Unfortunately, neither choice is a very good idea. Let me explain why.

One side argues that the tuition system still works because over the course of a lifetime, college graduates earn significantly more than people who did not attend college. This group might argue this point by presenting data from the Bureau of Labor Statistics which claims a person with a high school diploma earns about $712 a week (37k/yr.), while an individual with a bachelor's degree earns $1,173 a week (61k/yr.).[62] This suggests someone who has a bachelor's earns roughly 65% more a year than someone who has a high school diploma.

However this information can be misleading. While it is true that in the past people with four-year degrees earned more than people with a high school diploma, this may not apply to the future. This statistic fails to factor in majors, the time spent to get a degree and the loans taken out to pay for it. This data is also unable to predict future job markets, future earnings, and fails to show the time it will take to get to someone's peak earning potential and the additional taxes someone would owe should they earn a higher income.

If someone earns $10 an hour and decides to leave their job to take out a loan which equates to $400 per month (close to U.S. average as shown in chapter 3) are they really at an advantage if they graduate and start making $14 an hour? Going to college to make 40% more seems like a great idea. A full-time worker making $10 an hour in California would bring home about $1,360 after taxes per month. A person working a full-time job making $14 an hour would bring home about $1,850 but would still owe on the college loans, meaning they would actually bring home $1,450. Was it worth the five or six years of not working, or taking a reduction of hours to get a degree where you benefit by less than $100 a month? This should go to prove that college grads aren't always in a better situation than nongrads and early in their career, many college grads are poorer than high school graduates due to their increased overhead from college loans and time spent learning when they could have been earning. It is the short-term struggles of these young people that is concerning.

However the long-term is also uncertain. Just because you have a degree doesn't mean you are guaranteed a huge financial advantage over someone who doesn't have one. When it comes to saving for retirement, an 18-year-old planning to retire at the age of 65, who has saved $5,000 for retirement and plans to contribute $200 a month will have $709,671 upon retirement assuming a 6% rate of return. Someone who starts saving at the age of 24 because they were going to college will have $483,497 using the same assumptions. In this case the worker that started earlier is expected to receive over $200,000 more in retirement.

If the tuition system is not changed in the United States, young people will continue to struggle with college debts and universities will continue to be incentivized to overcharge and keep people far beyond four years. Perhaps this isn't the best for the country.

Many who disagree with our current tuition system argue that college should be free. But a "free" education just means higher taxes. France, Germany, Sweden, and Finland are all known for their free education and all of them have a higher personal income tax rate than the U.S. However none of these nations have a higher percent of the population with degrees than the U.S. As of 2017, 46% of people in the U.S. go on to obtain degrees while only 29% graduate college in Germany, 35% in France, 44% in Finland and 42% in Sweden.[63]

Low graduation rates in countries like Germany and France can be explained by their strict testing requirements. Not everyone who wants to get a degree can have one if they don't qualify. If you want to study at a German university, you will need a

"Hochschulzugangsberechtigung"—or "university entrance qualification". This is a school-leaving certificate which qualifies you for university study. If your secondary-school certificate is deemed insufficient for study in Germany, you will have to attend a foundation course ("Studienkolleg") before you are allowed to enroll.[64]

In France young people are required to take the baccalauréat exam. The bac is a weeklong process that includes written and oral tests in everything from French literature to math to philosophy. And unlike the SAT, the bac is the sole factor that determines whether a French student will graduate from lycée; grades and extracurricular activities are not considered.[65]

The greatest challenge in terms of free education would be implementation. The U.S. would struggle to implement this system because of how much the United States spends per student and how our capitalistic system with high military expenditures forces lower spending on social programs.

When it comes to higher education spending it was estimated in 2015 that it cost $31,000 per full-time-equivalent (FTE) student in the United States. This is almost twice the cost of France or Germany where the cost is $16,300 and $17,400 respectively. The only country that is close to the spending of the U.S. is Sweden which spends $25,100.[66] However the U.S. spends 3.2% of its GDP on military while Sweden spends only 1%.[67] This will be talked about in greater detail in a later chapter.

The reality is that if the U.S. were to attempt to introduce a free education system they would need to limit who would qualify for it resulting in a smaller population percentage of people with college degrees. It would also require a significant amount of government spending to be focused on education that currently has other purposes. Free education isn't a great answer to our current higher education woes.

There is a third option that is perhaps better than our current system and less problematic than implementing free college. This system would aim at fixing the higher education system by changing the incentives that govern it. This can be done by applying two changes. The first change is to force tuition to be collected after graduation. The second change would be to make tuition proportional to a graduate's take-home paycheck. For example, if someone goes to college for four years, they should pay (15% or some other realistic percentage) of their wages after college for four years toward the institution they attended. This could be policed by a government agency or consumer banking company such as Sallie Mae. Currently we have a system where institutions and debt determine the price of higher education. The system I suggest makes obtaining quality jobs and monetary achievement the determining factor in price. In my proposed solution, tuition acts kind of like a temporary tax instead of a burden that turns young people into debt slaves.

The system I have suggested could be used to put pressure on colleges to get students to graduate in four years as there is no longer an incentive to keep them there. It also forces colleges to teach students better work-related skills so that they would get better jobs. Thus, the institution would make more money. This would help to make society more productive and strengthen skillsets in the job market. Colleges would still have complete control over who gains entry into their institution, but would only select those who have the most upside earning potential. This system would also provide more opportunity to people who grew up poor and put everyone on an equal playing field. Low value degrees would be phased out, because if the degrees don't earn the student any money, the colleges would stop teaching them in favor of degrees that receive a better return on investment. Degrees would also tend to evolve to mimic the skills needed in the free market. This system also wouldn't demand a massive increase in taxes which "Free" education would.

Although a perfect higher education system is unobtainable, there are many ways that it can be improved. There are also other options such as trade schools and apprenticeship programs which can provide a more affordable or more focused skillset to set someone on a more concrete career path. It is also important to understand that some people are not well suited to pursue a four-year degree. When it comes to universities, solving problems starts with taking action. Taking action requires people who aren't afraid to fail. Those are the people who are the future of this country.

CHAPTER 6

The Challenge of Minimum Wage

The National Low Income Housing Coalition reports that a full-time worker earning the federal minimum wage of $7.25 would need to work approximately 122 hours per week for all fifty-two weeks of the year, or approximately three full-time jobs, to afford a two-bedroom rental home at the 2016 national average fair market rent.[68] Minimum wage is not designed to provide people with an extravagant lifestyle, but people making minimum wage today have far lower living standards than in years past. According to the U.S. Bureau of Labor Statistics, in 2017, there were 1.8 million workers with wages at or below the federal minimum wage that made up 2.3% of all hourly paid workers.[69] As rent and cost of living continues to rise throughout the United States, many observing this problem have suggested increasing minimum wage as a solution. But does raising minimum wage really solve this issue?

Minimum wage jobs were never intended to be careers. They were intended to be stepping stones for low skilled workers or young people getting their first job in high school. However, in today's age, an increasing number of Americans are staying at minimum wage jobs longer, and are older than the minimum wage workers from previous generations. Fivethirtyeight.com ran a study that compared minimum wage workers from 1995 and 2014. This study found during the strong labor market of the mid-1990s, only 1 in 5 minimum-wage workers was still earning minimum wage a year later, in 2014, that number was nearly 1 in 3. Furthermore, the study also found that during this time period there was a large decrease of workers aged 16–19 and a considerable increase in those aged 20 to 54.[70]

Is it moral for someone to work a full-time 40-hour job and not be able to afford to raise a family? Is it moral to keep people at the same wage for years? The short answer is no, but very few if any businesses actually care. In fact, CEOs and owners of companies have a legal obligation to shareholders to try and maximize their value on all companies traded on the stock exchange, which in many cases promotes acting against morality. The vast majority of big businesses do not care about morality, they care about profits, and there's nothing wrong with that, we live in a capitalistic society. But an argument could be made that these huge profits are hurting low skilled workers.

The federal government established a minimum wage in a 1938 law called the Fair Labor Standards Act. On October 24, 1938, a 25-cent an hour minimum wage went into effect. The minimum wage reached its (inflation-adjusted) historic high in 1968, at the rate of $1.60 per hour. $1.60 an hour in 1968 would be equivalent to $11.87 per hour in 2018 dollars according to the CPI.[71] Considering the current federal minimum wage is $7.25 per hour, those working minimum wage jobs today are making approximately 61% ($7.25/$11.87) of what minimum wage workers made in 1968. However, as demonstrated in the second chapter of this book, there are many costs that have greatly surpassed the CPI and inflation, making these economic rulers poor reference points. The argument can be made that someone working a minimum wage job today could in fact be making half or less than half of what a minimum wage worker made in the 1960s.

Seeing this drastic decrease in purchasing power has led some economists to suggest indexing minimum wage by mean real economic growth, which is a credible argument. Many believe that the minimum wage should be linked to the median standard cost of living for each generation, not just the Consumer Price Index or inflation.

Right now, there is a big push for $15 an hour minimum wage. As crazy as it sounds, a $15 minimum wage would give more than half of American workers a raise. As stated in a previous chapter the current median income in the United States is $14.42 an hour, meaning 50% of the population makes more and 50% makes less. Why should we stop at $15 an hour, though? Why not $20 an hour or $25 an hour minimum wage?

As great as upping the minimum wage sounds, it would price many lower wage earners out of the market. If minimum wage is raised too high, people will lose their jobs, get their hours cut or be forced onto government programs in the form of welfare. The middle class will end up paying for this mistake in the form of increased taxes which will ultimately make them poor as well. People need to realize, raising the current minimum wage from $10 to $15 does not mean the people currently making $15 will also receive a raise. As a worker, it would be illegal for you to work for wages that are lower than the minimum, even if you desperately needed the money and didn't have a job. Personally, I have a hard time believing that a grocery store would be willing to pay someone $15 an hour to bag groceries.

Many states currently have a minimum wage that is above the federal requirement of $7.25 an hour. In most cases these states set minimum wage around $10. If minimum wage is raised to $15 an hour this would result in at least a 50% increase for the cost of low skill labor. This would hurt smaller businesses who simply cannot afford such a drastic wage increase. A small business that has ten employees would only be able to support about six if wages increased in such a way. This would create pressure on employees to work harder and have more responsibilities. Some small companies may go out of business entirely if their margins are not high enough on their services or products.

Three years ago, the city of Seattle voted to gradually raise its minimum wage to $15 an hour. According to a study by the University of Washington, it has been found that by raising the minimum wage, fewer hours are being given to lower skilled workers. Studies found that when wages were raised to $13 an hour, employers cut hours by 9% which resulted in a monthly compensation drop of roughly $125 per worker.[72] This wage hike results in $100M a year in lost payroll for low earners. This study shows that forcing businesses to pay more for labor hurts the very people that it is designed to help. Interestingly enough, most programs that are built to help poor people actually end up doing just the opposite, and in fact make everyone poor in the long run. Seattle's experiment provides great insight into the unintended consequences of raising minimum wage.

Any benefits of raising the minimum wage are only temporary. While in the short-term, higher wages would lead to less financial stress on workers, in the medium and long term it will cause more outsourcing to foreign countries and fewer jobs or fewer hours for workers here in the United States. Prices of goods and services within the area would, in all likelihood, increase as a result of the increased cost of labor. This would mean that if you did manage to earn a higher income, that higher income would be offset by higher costs of goods and services.

Raising minimum wage also puts pressure on companies to act in ways that hurt low income workers. One way companies deal with increased costs is to eliminate jobs through the use of robotics and modern technology. While this will happen regardless of minimum wage, the higher costs associated with lower skilled labor is leading to an increased speed in which robotics are being developed and replacing people. In 2017, the restaurant chain Wendy's added self-service ordering kiosks to over 1,000 restaurants, or about 15% of its stores.[73] These kiosks allow diners to order without help from behind-the-counter workers. Panera Bread aims to add touch-screen kiosks to all its restaurants within a few years, and McDonald's wants kiosks where diners can customize their burgers at each of its U.S. locations. A restaurant chain called CaliBurger developed Flippy the burger robot. Yes, there is a place where you can get a burger made by a robot. However, robots are not just limited to fast-food. Many are also replacing workers in assembly factories and robotics are also being developed to take jobs in industries such as hospitality, transportation and storage. Companies are by nature designed to try and keep worker overhead as low as possible. The use of robotics is a great way to eliminate low-skilled labor.

Another way companies combat the cost of low skilled labor is to hire illegal immigrants to fill positions. Again, this will happen regardless of minimum wage, but higher costs motivate companies to hire more workers that are paid under the table. According to the Pew research center, there were ten and a half million unauthorized immigrants in the U.S. in 2017. The majority of illegal immigrants are Mexicans (Approximately 47% in 2017)[74] Blacks and Hispanics are the people who tend to lose the most from this situation due to the increased competition for low wage jobs. While hiring undocumented workers is illegal, that doesn't stop companies from doing it.

In 2001, Tyson Foods Inc., the nation's largest meat producer and processor, was indicted for the smuggling of illegal immigrants into the U.S. to work at their plants.[75] In 2012, a natural food company in Gridley, California, Mary's Gone Crackers, Inc. paid

$1.5 million to avoid prosecution for hiring forty-nine illegal aliens. The company rehired thirteen of the illegal alien employees after the ICE audit that originally busted them.[76] In 2006 Crider Inc., a chicken processing plant in Georgia, was raided by immigration agents, and 75% of its workforce vanished over a single weekend. Shortly after, Crider placed an ad in the local newspaper announcing job openings at higher wages.[77] There are dozens of major companies that have, and continue to rely on, illegal immigrants to keep labor costs down. Some people argue that illegal immigrants are a positive to the economy because they do a lot of jobs that no one else would do. The reality is that they are a major net negative on the economy.

The predicament that minimum-wage workers face is tough. They can't really survive on current wages, but higher wages might cost them their jobs. Several states have adopted or proposed multi-tier minimum wage systems to try and diminish the negative effects associated with minimum wage increases. Some believe that age should affect rates, while others believe population density or offered benefits should have an impact on wages. There are also people who argue for a minimum wage system based on levels of higher education.

Many believe that younger workers under the ages of 18 or 21 should have a lower minimum wage requirement because they bring fewer skills to the workforce or that they still live with their parents. This is also branded as a solution to high unemployment rates among young people. This may result in more young people taking jobs because they will have more opportunity, or it may result in more young people not working because the pay is less, and instead they would focus their attention on education. A potential issue associated with this idea is that employers will start to hire many more young people because it will save them money. This could cause problems if people in their 20s and 30s and thirties with children are priced out of the job market and unable to help support their families. In addition, the question would arise whether this was age discrimination or not.

Michigan currently offers a tiered minimum wage system where minors under 18 are paid 85% of the minimum hourly wage and newly hired employees age 16 to 19 are allowed to be paid $4.25 per hour for the first 90 days of employment.[78] According to the bureau of labor statistics, in 2017, workers in the U.S. as a whole from ages 16–19 had a 14% unemployment rate. In the state of Michigan, people age 16–19 have a 13.7% unemployment rate. However, despite the fact that Michigan has a slightly lower unemployment for these young workers, their unemployment among people aged 20–24 is more than 2% higher than the national average.[79] Higher unemployment among 20–24 year olds in Michigan might be explained by this system promoting a revolving door policy. Once young workers reach their late teens or early 20s, companies are incentivized to replace them with a new crop of minors to save money with low-skill labor. However, the idea of a wage system where minors are paid slightly less may hold merit because it will give more young people practical skills which are greatly lacking in the higher education system.

Another proposed solution to the minimum wage dilemma is setting minimum wage according to population density. The idea for this system is based on the fact that rural areas tend to struggle with wage increases. This type of system is being introduced in Oregon from 2016 to 2022, where there are different minimum wages based on population density of your work location. Oregon is being broken up into three divisions: Standard, Portland Metro and Nonurban Counties. By July 1st, 2022 Portland Metro will be $1.25 over the standard minimum wage and nonurban counties will be $1 less than the standard minimum wage, this means that there will be a $2.25 per hour difference in minimum wage between these two areas.[80] This is an interesting and largely experimental process being introduced by Oregon, which may promote businesses to move into more rural areas, or incentivize workers to find jobs in the city. It's currently unclear what type of impact this type of system will have on the state's economy.

Nevada is currently working on a tiered minimum wage system based on offered benefits. Those companies that do not offer benefits will be required to pay a higher minimum wage.[81] Health insurance has long been a hot button issue in the U.S., and many believe that health care can be greatly improved or changed to benefit the community. Many U.S. employers use part-time workers as a way to avoid paying for insurances, and many simply deny all workers any type of benefits. I myself have struggled to have health insurance for much of my adult life due to working for lower quality companies and making slightly too much to get on government programs that supply free or subsidized insurances. I support Nevada's idea, and believe that all workers should be able to afford at least basic health insurance.

Lastly, there are those who believe in a system where people with degrees should have a higher minimum wage. Currently this has not been implemented by any states. It is thought that this would reduce the number of educated individuals hired by employers. If we enact a system that is based upon education, employers may start to hire less educated people, making a degree worth less. In my chapter on education I purpose a modified tuition system that is based on wage after graduation. I believe that this purposed solution is far better than a multi-tier minimum wage system based on education.

While raising the minimum wage or using a tiered minimum wage system has gained popularity, there are also those who wish to get rid of the minimum wage system entirely. Libertarians such as

Ron Paul often point to successful free market countries such as Switzerland where workers are among the highest paid in world earnings, yet there is no minimum wage. Another great example is that of Singapore. Both of these countries have vastly different financial structure and government than the United States and are very difficult, if not impossible to compare. One important factor is that the U.S. spends roughly 60 times more money on military than Singapore and roughly 120 times more money on military than that of Switzerland.[82] In Singapore, the largest shareholder of any given company is the government, not the people. While there is no minimum wage, the Singaporean government provides stimulus to give employees more money. The unemployment in Singapore is just 2.2%, yet there are still many people struggling with poverty.

According to Dr. Ralph Segalman, Switzerland is very different in the way they handle social programs. Many social programs are the responsibility of the community and not the government. Disability insurance is strictly defined in a way that it does not become an alternative to work. Switzerland believes in providing temporary help rather than creating dependency and tries as hard as possible to encourage the poor to help themselves. The Swiss also have very strict immigration control in an effort to reduce poverty. Their view is that they cannot provide for everyone in the world, or even for everyone who seeks to come to Switzerland so they need to be very careful on whom they let in.[83]

A free market system where there is bidding and selling of labor without a minimum wage is probably the best system achievable, however it would be extremely difficult, if not impossible to successfully implement this system in the United States. The surplus of labor in our country would drive wages downward in a free market. A free market system only works if people won't just take any job presented to them. Unfortunately, in today's economy people are so desperate, and there are so few employment opportunities that many will take any job they can get.

As for the minimum wage debate, there are two camps of people: the people arguing for a higher wage, and the people who believe it should stay the same. Perhaps there is another option.

The real problem is not that minimum wage is too low; it is that it cannot buy enough. Rather than bring wages up, what would happen if there was an effort to bring costs down? Some of the largest culprits hurting minimum wage workers are high rent prices, debt, and concentration of the population. What would happen if there was an effort to reduce costs in these areas? How would one achieve this?

One of the biggest challenges is the high cost of rent. This is especially prevalent in more populous states like California, New York, Illinois and Florida. I live in San Diego, and it has been proposed to loosen San Diego granny flat rules so that rent prices will go down. Unfortunately, this only acts as a temporary solution until more people decide they want to move here. This doesn't solve the underlying problem. The main reason the price of housing is so high is debt. Longer term mortgages such as the 30-year mortgage and larger mortgages such as the jumbo mortgage push the prices of housing much higher than the actual value due to creating more demand. Today's financing options, which were once designed to help poor people, are now creating great difficulty for members of the poor and middle classes. If we eliminated or decreased debt and mortgage terms, the prices would go drastically lower. For example, if we banned mortgage terms over 15-year durations, fewer people would qualify for these loans and the price of real estate would go down. Not everyone needs to own a house.

Population density presents another unique challenge. Currently, approximately 323 million people live in America. Although we have 50 states, approximately 122 million people or nearly 40% of the American population live in just five of these states.[84] If the population could be distributed more evenly across the U.S., the prices of rent could become more affordable. So what do these five states have that make people want to live there? Weather, technology, infrastructure, beaches and entertainment tend to be some of the greatest attractors to a state. It is not possible for people to change weather or beaches, but people can create better technology, infrastructure and entertainment, which are three things lacking in many areas of the United States. Geographic areas such as the Midwest have some of the least population-dense states in the country, and also some of the poorest technology, infrastructure and entertainment.

I lived in Fayetteville, Arkansas for a brief period of time in 2016 to take a job. When I arrived, I remember feeling as though I had been teleported back to 1990. The weather was quite different from what I was used to, but perhaps the biggest challenge was the slower pace of life and the lack of modern technology and infrastructure. Truthfully, there wasn't a lot to do, there were no concerts by famous artists, no pro sports teams, few museums, no cybercafés, no nightclubs and no real innovation to be found. If Fayetteville had just a few of the things I had mentioned, it would attract a great many more people to the city. The challenge is that in the United States there is the choice between excitement and being poor, or having money and being bored. If the United States offered incentives in the form of tax breaks, or promoted higher education for people from less developed states to develop them, it could help to spread out the population and thus lower the prices of rent because the demand would be reduced.

In 2016, as part of its mission to educate business leaders to solve society's most pressing problems, Stanford Graduate School of Business established a fellowship to provide financial support for up to three students with a passion for generating economic development in regions of the U.S. under-represented in the MBA program. These scholarships would go to students hailing from Midwest origins.[85] I applaud Stanford for doing this, and hope that more colleges will aim to improve less advanced parts of the country.

Another way to bring costs down is for the government to lower taxes. Unfortunately, one of the reasons why taxes are so high is because of government programs like Medicare, Medicaid and social security which combine to eat up 66% of the budget every year. Lowering taxes on things like gas would help to make transportation costs cheaper and help to push prices lower in a competitive industry. The government could also offer technology upgrades as subsidies to increase production and efficiency which would help to lower costs. An example would be to help farmers save money by giving them Tree Teepees, a product that saves many gallons of water by concentrating the water around trees and reducing waste water to areas that don't need it.

Aiming to introduce more efficiency and better systems would help competing firms be able to further lower their prices if they were not a monopoly or oligopoly. This would help increase purchasing power for people making minimum wage and hopefully remove some of the stress and burdens of being in the lower class. If we can help to eliminate poverty at the bottom level we can remove people from government programs that create dependency. Giving opportunities to people can help the economy and save taxpayers money. At the same time, we should not put all the focus on the lower class. Perhaps even more important is the middle class, and they need help too.

CHAPTER 7

Poor Hiring Practices and the Disappearing Middle Class

The majority of economists tie the health of the middle class to the growth of the economy and the quality of government. "Middle Class" is a term that is used broadly to define people who are financially better off than the poor, but not quite as well off as the rich. It is quite difficult to define what exactly constitutes a member of the middle class.

If you look online, you will find a hundred definitions, formulas and wages for what "Middle Class" is. In recent years more people are claiming that the middle class is declining and that there is a steep rise in the number of poor people. Is this accurate information or is this an excuse that people are using to make themselves feel better about their own shortcomings?

What percent of people in America can we consider middle class and above, and how much larger has the poor class grown in the last twenty years? If the middle class is disappearing, how can it be measured? There needs to be a quantifiable method to see what exactly is going on. I believe the best way to do this is to define middle class based on their purchasing power of housing. Owning a house is generally the largest expenditure people make in their lifetime and acts as a great milestone to measure progress by.

I define a member of the middle class as someone who can meet two different metrics. Firstly, a person who is middle class should be able to buy a house in their area without a mortgage after saving for fifteen years. Secondly, someone in the middle class will be able to save about one third of their wage if they are responsible. Using these two metrics, someone who is middle class or better can be defined by 1/3 wage * 15. For example, if the average house costs $150,000 in your area, a middle class person would need to make at least $30,000 per year or more. (30000 * .33) * 15 = 150,000. This might be considered by some to be subjective, but using this method can help to give an idea of just how much of the middle class has disappeared in recent years. Note: this chapter uses the years 2015 and 1995 for reference points to give people a better idea of what has happened in the last twenty years.

To find out how many people represent the middle class using my formula, both wages and home prices must be included. The Social Security Administration currently has wage statistics available online from the years 1989 to 2015. These statistics show the number of people and the cumulative portion of the population that make salary brackets in $5k increments from $0–$200,000 per year. Median sales prices of new houses in the United States can be found using the Federal Reserve Bank of St. Louis. Their data spans from 1963 to 2018.

FRED reports that in January of 1995, the median sales price of a new house was $127,900, and in January of 2015, the median sales price of a new house was $292,000.[86] Using the formula previously provided, a person must have made more than $25,000 per year in 1995 to be considered middle or upper class. In 2015, someone would need to have made more than $60,000 per year to be middle class.

The Social Security Administration shows that in 1995 66% of Americans made less than $25,000 a year and in 2015 approximately 77.3% of the population in the United States made less than

$60,000 per year.[87] This means that from 1995 to 2015 the middle and upper class retracted from roughly 34% to 22.7%, a reduction of more than 10% of the population in only 20 years. Considering our current population is about 321 million, this would amount to roughly 32 million people moving from middle or upper class to lower class.

How did this happen? The truth is that more than one thing has been responsible for this reduction. Some of the biggest culprits were older people working longer, staffing agencies, questionable hiring practices, immigration, the H1B visa and outsourcing. Each of these issues will be addressed and assessed during this chapter.

The first contributing factor to the shrinking middle class is older people who are staying in the work force longer. This isn't the older generation's fault. Older people are being forced to work longer largely because people are living longer and need more money in order to have a successful retirement. Since 1950, America has seen the life expectancy at birth increase from approximately 68 to 78, equating to an additional ten years of retirement. Pew Research reports that in May 2000, 12.8% of people older than the age of 65 held a job and by May 2016, the number had risen to 18.8%.[88] This is a contributing factor in making it harder to get entry level work experience for younger people. It also may be a cause of under-employment where younger workers with college degrees are forced into lower paying jobs.

Another challenge that many middle class workers are facing is staffing agencies. As an owner of a publicly traded company on the stock market, you have the obligation to maximize shareholder value. One tactic many larger companies are now using, is hiring staffing agencies and recruiters. According to the American Staffing Association, during the course of a year, America's staffing companies hire nearly 15 million temporary and contract employees. In addition, from 2001 to 2018 the annual totals for staffing and recruiting industry sales rose from $82 billion to $167 billion.[89] The U.S. Bureau of labor statistics reports that in January of 2018, the number of employed persons in the United States was approximately 154 million.[90] This means approximately 10% of the total workforce goes through a temp or contract agency.

Staffing agencies and recruiters might sound nice, but some act as parasites, destroying the middle class and artificially lowering wages. From my experience, this is especially true for staffing agencies coming out of India. A large company might be willing to spend $25 per hour on a great employee in a specific field, and they offer this wage to a staffing agency. In most cases the staffing agency does not charge for the use of their services from the large company, the staffing agency makes money by using recruiters to try and fill a position at a lower wage than the large company is willing to spend on the position. Staffing agencies act like middle men keeping the difference between the salary offered by the large company, and the salary offered to the employee. The employee, instead of making $25 an hour will make somewhere around $18. This means that the staffing agency is now making $7 an hour, for every hour that their new employee works. This gives birth to several questions.

While many staffing companies talk about terms like "getting your foot in the door" or "gaining valuable job experience" some can, in fact, make huge margins from their workers' hours. At what point is the staffing agency's profit margins from their workers considered taking advantage of them? Should we cap the margins that these companies make? Is it fair to take advantage of a desperate person who is trying to feed their family?

I worked a job as an outsourced contractor where I was making $50,000 a year. The staffing company I was working for charged $99,000 for my services. They then proceeded to negotiate $131,000 for my contract and refused to give me a raise to combat cost of living increases. My $50,000 a year job gave them $81,000 in profit.

Staffing agencies also hurt employees in three major ways besides a lower wage. First of all, the staffing agency will generally not disclose how much they are getting paid for the position you are working. This leaves workers to feel that they are of less value in the workplace than they are actually worth. Secondly, workers from staffing agencies can be treated differently than permanent workers and feel displaced as they can be excluded from company events or social gatherings. Lastly, staffing companies act as an additional step for many people as they work toward a decent job, when in the past most people received a great job out of college.

Different staffing agencies have different onboarding procedures and ways of conducting business. Some recruiters have quotas to set meetings that they are judged by, and some will contact you only to try and gain access to manager names at your current company in an attempt to grow their connections. Some require that you meet with them in person like a formal interview so they can submit you for a role. Other agencies require that you take skills tests for prospective jobs. Some agencies will simply get your information online and contact you to submit you for a role.

When staffing agencies submit you for a role you generally go into a smaller pile of résumés. However, each company tends to send multiple candidates for a single job and some require several hours of your time. It might not be worth it to spend several hours dealing with a recruiter for one position when you could fill out ten applications in the same amount of time?

One of the big problems is that as agencies have become an easier way to make money, more foreign companies are getting involved. Increased competition between staffing agencies is leading to laziness and sloppiness among recruiters. Most recruiters will simply take a pile of résumés and forward it somewhere else without offering any real value. Should these people make thousands of dollars for sending three emails?

Despite the downfalls of staffing agencies, many larger companies realized they could save money by cutting the size of their HR departments and replacing them with staffing agencies and recruiters. In many cases an employee can be hired on a temporary or contract basis, allowing larger companies to cheat good workers out of benefits such as health care. In addition, the staffing agencies, not the large companies, pay for unemployment, if after a job is completed a given employee is seen as being eligible.

Going through staffing agencies and also providing at-will employment has very little risk to employers as they can simply remove any employee at any time without addressing the employee face to face. The staffing agency will be the one to deliver the news. Temp, contract and staffing agencies also provide a great way to deliver budget cuts.

Another challenge that many middle class individuals are facing is the questionable hiring practices that have evolved in businesses over the past few decades. A lot of large corporations post "fake" jobs, and hold fake interviews with no intention to hire in the first place. There are several different incentives for doing this. Sometimes companies hold interviews due to laws or because company standards dictate that they engage in a certain number of interviews before they promote an internal candidate. They often try and rationalize that this internal candidate is better by benchmarking against others that have an inferior skillset. The decision on who they were going to hire was determined before they even looked at a single résumé.

Companies are also incentivized to engage in fake interviews to fool analysts and rating agencies to think that their company is doing really well and expanding. This can be achieved by posting on job boards, attending career fairs or hosting events that are really used for publicity more than anything else. Corporations have a very limited ability to manipulate their financial statements, but they can manipulate their headcount. Their goal is to trick analysts to assign higher valuation figures and higher price targets for their stocks.

Sometimes, fake interviews happen when hiring slows down. During hiring freezes and slowdowns, HR people begin to fear for their jobs and want to look as busy as possible. As a result, they interview hundreds of candidates for a single role or interview for jobs that don't actually exist.

Another way that corporations are winning in today's labor market is with employment at will. The concept of "employment at will" has become a more debated issue in the past few years. It originally became popular in the 1930s, giving employers the right to terminate employees at will, for any or no reason without providing specific protections such as prior warning, fair procedures, or an evaluation. Some people view this concept as a way for employers to treat people like a property right and not like a human being. I have never understood the concept of giving "two weeks' notice" to an employer if that is not something that they would give me should they be planning to lay me off.

Graduating and trying to find a job in one of the most challenging economic recessions in history led me to take some less than reputable jobs. It was an employer's market and has continued to be for many years now. Working at these places I witnessed many interesting hiring practices in action. In one company where I worked, I watched them hire and fire for the same position four times in a period of several months. The managers kept citing that the people weren't a good fit, or that they were lazy, or that they weren't pulling their weight.

An intelligent person would see that in this situation the workers were not the core problem. In this case, the core problem was in all likelihood one of three things. The first possible explanation was that the company had poor hiring practices and was not finding employees with the correct skillsets. The second possibility was that the training provided for the job was poor and caused a poor worker performance. The third possibility was that the manager's expectations for the job were not clearly defined, and the employee did not understand what was asked of them. All three of these possibilities lead to the same conclusion: management was the problem, not the employee.

It's very easy for a company to churn through employees with the concept of at-will employment and a stack of 1000 résumés on a desk, but people are not interchangeable pieces of machinery. By exercising their right to hire and fire on a dime, companies often fail to realize their own shortcomings within their organization. It's very easy to blame others for lack of performance; it's hard to blame oneself. With an employer's market and a surge in at-will employment comes lower quality, or nonexistent training as well as reduced employee longevity.

Immigration is another challenge that the middle class is facing. Many people argue that immigration is actually a positive on both wages and the economy. They site famous immigrants like Arnold Schwarzenegger, Elon Musk, Sergey Brin, and Albert Einstein. There are also several studies that seem to suggest immigrants create more jobs than native born citizens. However, there are no studies that show the actual wages that these jobs create. According to American Community Survey (ACS), more than 43.7 million immigrants resided in the United States in 2016, accounting for 13.5% of the total U.S. population of 323.1 million.[91] This amounts to over 18 million immigrants in the last 20 years. If each of these legal immigrants had a job they would make up more than

10% of our entire work force. Breitbart claims that 75% of U.S. population growth since the year 2000 has come from immigration and the United States has the most immigrants of any country in the world.[92] Perhaps the most disturbing fact is that according to The U.S. department of labor, there is a higher unemployment rate among U.S. born citizens in comparison to foreign born citizens.[93] Why is this happening?

The main reason why foreigners have a lower unemployment rate than our citizens is that they can work for lower wages than people who grew up in the United States. This boils down to the relative costs between foreign workers and Americans. Foreigners have a comparative advantage. According to the New York Times, tuition at Dartmouth is $41,736 a year, not including room and board, while most of the colleges of Delhi University cost about $150 to $500 per year.[94] When college-educated immigrants come from India their overhead and loans are much lower than people from the United States, and thus they are able to work for a much lower wage. This constant unloading of foreigners also raises rent prices in areas by creating more demand. The failure in the U.S. education as a whole has made it almost impossible for Americans to compete for jobs in their own country. This is also the main reason why the H1B visa is such a problem.

Pew Research reports that The U.S. government approved more than 859,600 H1B visa applications in fiscal 2010–2016.[95] The introduction of the H1B visa aims to get educated foreigners over to the United States to work. These people take up middle- to high-level skill and income jobs. The bulk of H1B visas come from India, and the vast majority of these men and women work for tech and engineering companies. Although H1B workers make their companies great amounts of money in the short term by saving the company money on worker wages, they create significant damage in the long term. Firstly, most of the men and women who have an H1B Visa speak English as a second language, which leads to countless workplace errors due simply to translation problems. Second, the standards are different for earning a degree abroad compared to those of the U.S. In addition, there are cultural differences that affect expectations and general protocols for behavior.

Having educated workers from third world countries come to the United States also damages the countries that they came from. If all the intelligent people from a third world country leave, the country as a whole suffers. Instead of making their home country better by improving technology, infrastructure and other foundations for living, these countries just continue to become less and less habitable. The introduction of the H1B Visa is a net negative to the world and the U.S.

Another way that our companies hurt the middle class is through outsourcing. Outsourcing is more prevalent among larger corporations than small mom-and-pop establishments. When was the last time that you had a problem paying a bill, and you *didn't* speak to someone from a foreign country?

According to Statisticbrain, 2,382,000 jobs were outsourced from the United States in 2015 alone. San Jose, CA, and San Francisco, CA, have the highest numbers for outsourcing, which led to a loss of over $14.4 billion for American computer programmers and software engineers alone.[96] Keep in mind the number of employed persons in the United States is 152 million as stated in the last chapter. This means that outsourcing removes more than 1.5% of the jobs in the United States. For the United States to have a strong economy we must ban outsourcing.

Immigration, outsourcing and H1B visas all have one thing in common: they cost Americans jobs and wages. This raises many questions. Should the U.S. government continue to allow foreigners to receive jobs before American's who were born, worked and educated in America? Should the government have an obligation to its own people before foreigners? What most people fail to realize is that Americans will be the ones to make sacrifices for all of the workers from other countries who come here. It's important to realize that H1B Visa holders, outsourcing, temp jobs and contract agencies result in millions of jobs being affected where either wages are reduced or Americans are being replaced by foreign job seekers. There needs to be a greater effort placed on helping people in the United States. There is plenty of poverty here, we need to solve our own problems before helping those from other countries.

In the 1930s American comedian and commentator Will Rogers coined the phrase Trickle-down economics which is also known as trickle-down theory. He used this phrase to describe President Herbert Hoover's stimulus efforts during the Great Depression. The definition by Investopedia is that trickle-down theory argues for income and capital gains tax breaks or other financial benefits to large businesses, investors and entrepreneurs in order to stimulate economic growth.[97] The argument hinges on two assumptions: all members of society benefit from growth; and growth is most likely to come from those with the resources and skills to increase productive output.

Much of the economy is determined by motivation and people acting in their own best interest. The problem with Trickle-down economics is that almost all people are motivated by self-interest. It is a survival strategy built into our DNA. There is no motivation to use extra money saved by tax breaks or other financial benefits on employees. Instead, Trickle-down economics just makes big businesses richer. Without their greed, people like Jeff Bezos wouldn't have close to $150 billion.

I believe in what I like to call *Steam Up Economics*. Remove the sources that are destroying the middle class and the problems hurting low income workers, so that people will have more opportunities for better wages and opportunities.

CHAPTER 8

Questions You Should Be Asking About Taxes

The greatest way to create extreme change is to go about it so slowly that no one notices. People just accept it as the way it has always been. The first 130 years or so of the United States were characterized by low tax rates; few new major taxes were introduced. In the early 1900s things began to change and America started to go tax crazy.

In 1913, the United States introduced income taxes and capital gains taxes. A few years later in 1916, the Modern Estate tax was introduced. The 1930s saw the creation of sales taxes and gas taxes, and in the late 1950s the hotel tax was introduced. Today we are paying many times more taxes than people just one hundred years ago. As times become harder for Americans, we need to ask ourselves: at what point have taxes gone too far?

The vast majority of Americans have little to no knowledge about taxes and where their tax dollars go. In many cases they are completely reliant upon tax professionals to compute their taxes. This chapter aims to bring up important questions about taxes and will focus on why the systems that govern the collection of several taxes are inherently flawed and dangerous to the future of the economy. This chapter will be broken up into two sections. The first part of this chapter will focus on federal taxes while the second part will focus on state taxes. Some taxes such as income taxes and capital gains are taxed at both the state and the federal level.

The two greatest sources of tax revenue for the federal government are income taxes and payroll taxes. Income taxes accounted for roughly 47% of federal tax revenue in 2016, while payroll taxes were responsible for approximately 34% of federal tax revenue.[98] In 1990, the federal government brought in more than $1 trillion in tax revenue for the first time. In 2019, they brought in $3.46 trillion.[99] Why did citizens pay nearly twice the inflation adjusted taxes to the federal government in 2019 in comparison to 1990? Have our government programs become twice as expensive, or is this just evidence that our government has a spending problem?

One of our country's greatest problems lies with the federal income tax. The federal income tax was enacted in 1913 to help finance World War I. At the time there were seven tax brackets which varied from 1% to 7%.[100] The establishment of more government programs such as welfare and social security in the 1930s led to steep increases in taxes. By 1944, there were 24 tax brackets which ranged from 23% to 94%. Imagine paying 94¢ in taxes for every dollar you earned. Under the 2018 Trump tax plan, there are seven tax brackets which range from 10% to 37%. While our current tax system is not as expensive as it has been, it equates to a tenfold increase in the amount of taxes paid by poor people and more than five times the tax burden for the rich since the federal income tax was introduced in 1913.

The United States has a progressive tax system. This means that people who earn more money go into higher tax brackets where they pay higher amounts of taxes and a higher percent of their income. The idea behind a progressive tax system is the ability-to-pay-principle. This principle acts to address economic inequalities in society and claims that people who make less money can't afford to pay taxes without sacrificing basic needs such as medical care, quality food, vehicle repair, and access to higher education. Since middle-

and upper-class individuals make more money, they have their basic needs met, and thus should be the ones responsible to pay the majority of taxes.

Perhaps one of the worst issues with progressive taxes is that they do not factor in the number of hours that an individual or a family spends working. Some people work far longer hours in the effort to obtain a better quality life for themselves and their families. In essence, the people that tend to work longer hours tend to earn more money, but at the same time they also are forced to pay more taxes. Should harder working people be punished for their efforts? Is a system that pulls people down acceptable, rather than one that rewards those who have put in more time and energy? As it currently stands, income taxes act as a sort of punishment on success.

In addition to neglecting to look at hours worked, our progressive tax system also fails to factor in overhead appropriately. Chapter 4 briefly looked at overhead challenges in America, which are mainly determined by cost of living and debt. In significantly more expensive states with higher rent costs, would it make sense for lower taxes?

Our progressive tax system also ignores college loans which damages citizens who seek to obtain middle income and high-skilled jobs. Progressive taxes hurt younger people who aim to become doctors, lawyers, engineers, project managers, surgeons and dentists. These higher income professions have a very high barrier to entry and require significantly more education and financial investment. While doctors or engineers may earn significantly more money than other professionals, we often overlook the fact that they have staggering amounts of debt. Currently, the maximum student loan interest deduction can only lower your taxable income by up to $2,500 a year. This seems hardly fair considering many people who aim to obtain upper level professions have hundreds of thousands in debt.

The Association of American Medical Colleges reports that the average medical school debt balance for graduating physicians in 2016 was $190,000.[101] This doesn't even include the costs of an undergrad degree. The total average student loan balance for a doctor is approximately $220,000. For a loan this size, a 30-year repayment plan at 7% interest would cost $1464 a month for a total of $527,040. Yes, you read that correctly, your average doctor will need to pay back roughly half a million dollars in debt. Another thing to consider is that it takes between 11 and 14 years of higher education to become a physician. Is it appropriate that we should punish these individuals who worked extremely hard and went deep into debt? Who can give a rational argument for why physicians are forced to pay more than 15 times the taxes of your average citizen? Our system should motivate young people to become doctors, not deter them to engage in other professions that require less education.

Motivation is an extremely important factor in America. Middle-class individuals are finding progressive taxes hurt them when they are trying to move up in the world. Many find that getting a job with a higher wage can sound great, but that higher wage often leads to an extremely marginal increase in their standard of living. A person increasing their income from $35,000 to $45,000 will pay nearly $4,000 more in taxes a year. Is the excessive effort to climb to a better job worth it considering the added pressure and sacrifices? Should a small business spend extra time and energy to make more money when most of it will just evaporate in the form of taxes?

For the last several years the news media and the Democratic Party have continually complained that the rich do not pay enough in taxes, and that it is time for the rich to "pay their fair share." As mentioned earlier in the chapter, as of 2018, there are seven tax brackets which range from 10% to 37%. According to the IRS, people filing single in the lowest tax bracket who earn $0–$9,525 per year pay 10% of taxable income. In the second lowest bracket people who earn $9,526–$38,700 pay $952.50 *plus* 12% of the amount over $9,525. At the highest bracket where people earn $500,001 or more they are taxed $150,689.50 *plus* 37% of the amount over $500,000.[102]

As mentioned in earlier chapters the median income earner in the U.S. earns just $30,000 per year, which would put them in the second lowest bracket. An earner who grosses $30k will be taxed at 10% for the first $9,525 of their earnings which is $952.50. They will then be taxed at 12% of the remaining $20,475 of their earnings. This results in approximately $3409.50 in federal income taxes. In comparison, a person making $500,001 will be taxed 150,589.50. In this case a person in the highest taxed bracket will pay 44 times more in taxes than someone making the median income in America.

According to Pew Research the top 0.1% of earners in America pay 20.4% of all federal income tax and the top 1% of earners pay 38.3% of all federal income taxes. Furthermore, the poorest 43.8% of Americans pay only 1.4% of all federal income taxes.[103] Should the top 1% be paying nearly 30 times more in total taxes than the bottom 43.8%? The reality is that the rich pay an absurd amount in taxes every year. If people should bring up the argument that the rich need to "pay their fair share," the rich should actually be paying significantly less.

Progressive income taxes are clearly unfair and a net negative on the middle and upper classes in America. They are also overly complex. There are thousands of pages of tax codes and many people aren't aware of tax credits they could utilize to save money. Filing taxes should be a quick, simple, painless experience, yet it costs U.S. taxpayers 6.1 billion hours and $168 billion dollars per year.[104] Wouldn't a flat tax system where everyone paid 15% of their wage be a huge improvement on what we currently have? Why doesn't everyone pay a set amount of taxes like $3000 a year? If we want a system that is simple, efficient and fair why not have a flat tax system or a set amount of taxes?

While income taxes have become a huge problem, another questionable tax system is that of capital gains. This is a system that is taxed on both a state and federal level. In a nutshell, this tax is applied when something you invested in or your property is sold for a net gain on what you originally paid for it. The issue with this system is that it punishes people who take risks that benefit the economy.

Imagine that someone invests in a company that is traded on the stock market. Their investment helps to create jobs and growth for that company and the economy. If the company does well, they will make money on their investment and pay taxes on their gains, but if the company fails they will lose everything. In other words, someone takes a risk and they are punished for winning and for losing. It would make more sense to eliminate this tax in an effort to motivate people to put their money back into the businesses and economy of America.

While the majority of this chapter so far has focused on taxes coming from the federal government, there are also major issues associated with state specific taxes. The two major state taxes to discuss are sales tax and property taxes. Every state has a different sales tax percentage; some do not have sales tax at all. I like to use California as an example, as that is the state that I currently live in. In California there is an 8.25% sales tax which means for every dollar spent 8¼¢ go back to the government in the form of taxes. 6¢ from the 8¼¢ go into the state general fund.[105]

In 2017 approximately 70% of the state general fund went towards health and human services and K–12 education.[106] Money that goes towards health and human services provides Medi-Cal health care coverage and social safety net programs. According to the LA Times, from 2014 to 2017 Medi-Cal enrollment surged by 5 million people to a total of 13.5 million under President Obama's Affordable Care Act.[107] Poverty is running rampant in California, and growing out of control. Remember that nothing is free and that someone always needs to pay for it.

As for education, California has roughly 6.2 million students in the K–12 system. According to the 2015 Census, California spent approximately $66 billion which averages to about $10,500 per student. This is actually slightly lower than the $11,392 national average but a significant increase from the $5,001 spent per student for the 1992–1993 calendar year.[108] Why are these costs getting so much higher?

718,000 students or 11% of the student population is on special education programs which cost roughly $12 billion a year.[109] From this information it can be concluded that California spends more than one and a half times more on special education children in comparison to that of regular students. From a financial standpoint, this does not make sense. In addition, the state also offers several classes that help to teach foreign parents English at the cost of your tax dollars. It could be argued that many states are very inefficient and downright irresponsible with their tax dollars when it comes to education. Do we really need such high levels of state taxes to support such wasteful programs?

Another challenge is that of property taxes. Property taxes in the United States originated during colonial times so they have been around for hundreds of years. However, they have evolved to contain a major systematic flaw that is acting as a time bomb. In each state, a tax appraiser determines the value of someone's house and then proceeds to multiply it by the state tax rate to determine how much someone owes in state taxes. The problem with this is that low interest rates create an incentive for people to buy houses, even those who cannot afford them. This creates an artificial demand to buy these houses, and prices rise, in which people need to have greater and greater amounts of debt. Thus, this financing system creates higher property taxes.

Each year, our government continues to grow larger and larger. With this growth comes inefficiencies and more debt. Our government keeps close tabs on its citizens, but who keeps tabs on the government? As spending problems become more apparent, which programs are we going to cut? As taxes get higher how will Americans fare with their smaller paychecks? These are important questions to ask as we witness a continuing decline in the standard of living.

CHAPTER 9

The Population Pyramid and Government Programs

The early 1900s brought great change to government programs. The Civil Service Retirement Act of 1920 was a major contributor to modern pension plans, and in the 1930s FDR introduced the "New Deal" which brought with it Social Security and many of our modern welfare programs. Social Security, welfare and pensions all have one thing in common: they are all centered on the idea of population pyramids. For Social Security, young people would support old people and welfare, the wealthy and middle class would support the poor. Pensions are heavily reliant on the continuing flow of tax dollars from working citizens to retirees and are highly reliant on profitable investments in the stock market and bond market.

Today, these social programs have a big impact on government spending and the economy. The challenge is that these programs have grown larger and more expensive and a smaller percentage of the population is supporting them. The Center on Budget and Policy Priorities reported that for the 2016 fiscal year, 24% of the federal budget, or $916 billion, was spent on Social Security. During the same year, 26% of the federal budget, or $1 trillion was spent between Medicare, Medicaid, the Children's Health Insurance Program (CHIP), and the Affordable Care Act (ACA).[110] These several government programs make up approximately half of the federal government's budget.

Social security seemed like a pretty amazing idea at the time it was created. The idea behind Social Security was that people would continue to have more and more children, and these children would work and pay taxes to supplement their parents' retirement. A group of four children could easily supplement the retirement of just two older people. The problem was that in the early 1970s people began to have significantly fewer children. A society that once observed 3½ children per woman now saw fewer than 2.[111] For the last 40–50 years the birth rate has stayed extremely low which has resulted in a radical shift in the population pyramid.

The population pyramid project looks at the U.S. population by ages between the years of 1950 to 2015, and uses an estimation method to predict the population of America all the way to the year 2100. While their statistics break down the population in five-year intervals, I have broken it down into five groups of 15-year intervals, which I believe makes the information easier to understand. This aims to show you that because we have a much older population of baby boomers, we are spending substantially more on Social Security.

In 1950, the total population of the United States was 157,813,040. By 2017, it had grown to 326,474,013. The charts on the following page show the percentage of population in each age range.[112] What once looked like a pyramid from about the 1950s to the 1970s now resembles something closer to a rocket. By 2030, it is estimated that people age 60+ will make up 26% of the population and people too young to work will be close to 20%. There are almost twice as many old people who are in retirement since 1950, and many fewer people being born.

Population by Age in 1950

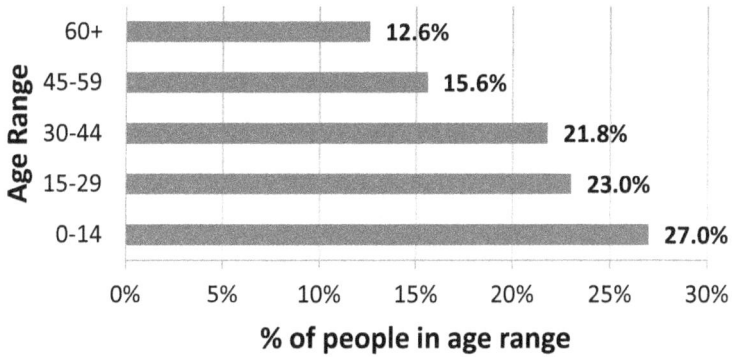

Age Range	%
60+	12.6%
45-59	15.6%
30-44	21.8%
15-29	23.0%
0-14	27.0%

% of people in age range

Population by Age in 2018

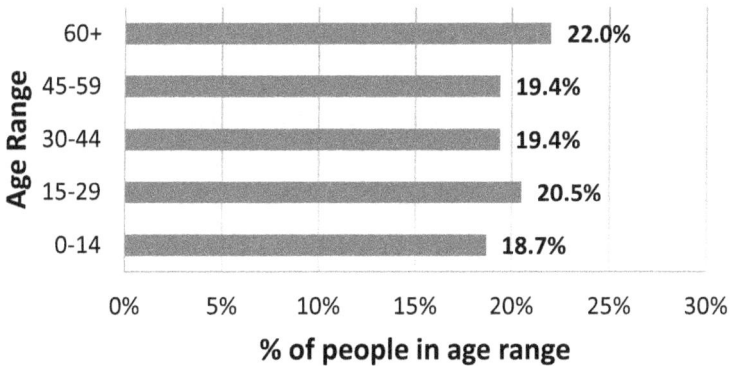

Age Range	%
60+	22.0%
45-59	19.4%
30-44	19.4%
15-29	20.5%
0-14	18.7%

% of people in age range

There are some major challenges ahead because of this shift in the pyramid. First, as more of this older generation enters retirement, these people will begin to withdraw their money from investments. This will result in more than $10 billion being taken out of the stock market and could result in a substantial loss in the value of stocks. Second, the fact that people are living longer combined with the threat of an aging population puts a lot of strain on social security benefits and government pensions. When Social Security began paying benefits in 1940, the average 65-year-old male had a period life expectancy of 11.9 years. By 2013, this figure had increased to 18 years, while the retirement age had increased by one year. This amounts to a 43% increase in the time spent collecting old-age benefits.[113]

When it was first introduced in 1935, Social Security was funded by a 1% tax for employers and employees on the first $3,000 of a worker's income. Today, this tax rate is approximately 6.2% on both employers and employees on up to $127,200.[114] The money the government collects in the form of taxes for Social Security goes to beneficiaries with the remainder going into the Social Security Trust Fund. This trust fund acts as a safety net if benefits exceed tax revenue. The problem is that Social security is soon set to go into an annual cash deficit, and current projections show that the Social Security trust fund will be out of money by the year 2034. This means that Social security will be entirely dependent on the money it takes in after 2034. People who attempt to retire after 2034 will in all likelihood receive much lower benefits (perhaps 70% or 60% of what they were promised) in order to fix this problem. It is inappropriate that newer generations are forced to pay higher taxes and receive fewer benefits from Social Security than previous genera-tions. Why are millennials left holding the bag? Unfortunately, Social Security has created poor spending habits and increased dependency among older generations, specifically the baby boomers when it comes to retirement.

Another major concern is Welfare. Welfare programs are govern-ment subsidies to the poor. In 2012, the census reported that about 21.3% or slightly more than 1/5 of the U.S. population is on at least one of these programs.[115] There are roughly 80 welfare programs, that together comprise the single largest item in the federal budget. Welfare was designed to assist people in poverty and make sure they received help at the expense of higher taxes of the middle and upper class. Welfare was built on the idea that the people who need help make up a very small portion of America. I like to view our welfare system like a giant cart. Suppose you have 100 people and 90 are pulling a cart with 10 inside that are unable to work. That would work just fine right? Now imagine 10 people trying to pull a cart with 90 inside. The issue is that participation in welfare programs has grown at a rate that exceeds population growth.

One of the largest welfare programs is SNAP. The U.S. Department of Agriculture, which oversees SNAP (food stamps), counted 42.3 million people on the program in 2017.[116] According to Statista spending on the SNAP program has increased from $18 billion in 2000 to $80 billion in 2015. This is more than twice as much inflation-adjusted money than was spent just 15 years prior.[117] As of August 2018, there were 66.6 million individuals enrolled in Medicaid in the United States.[118] According to Statista, the cost of Medicaid has increased from $159.5 billion to $549.1 billion from 1995 to 2015.[119] This is more than twice as costly to the government when inflation-adjusted compared to just 20 years ago.

In 2017, state and local government spending shows that nearly 1/3 of all welfare spending came from only two states. These two states were California and New York.[120] What's even more important is to understand the time period in which people are on government welfare programs. According to the census bureau, during 2012, 43% of people were on at least one major government assistance program. Furthermore, the average person on these programs was on them between 37 and 48 months (3–4 years).[115*] Welfare time limits differ by state and program, but 23 states have a five-year time limit. Others allow even longer.[121] In addition, many of these states allow extensions. There are circumstances that someone will need some extra help, but isn't five years of help a little excessive?

Many welfare recipients are promoted to stay on the programs as long as possible because of "The Welfare Cliff." This is the idea that earning even slightly more money may put you over the maximum gross income, making you ineligible for welfare programs. Mathematically, you would want to turn down these raises because the benefits you receive through welfare outweigh the potential raises.

According to Howard Baetjer Jr, a lecturer in the Department of Economics at Towson University, a single parent of two in Chicago is mathematically better off making $12 an hour than receiving a promotion to $15 an hour when on welfare programs. At $12 an hour a single parent of two in Chicago is eligible for refundable tax credits, food assistance, housing assistance, child care assistance, and medical assistance worth $41,465 combined. Coupling this assistance with the earned income of a $12 an hour job, which amounts to $22,121 after taxes, one would receive a combined total of $63,586 a year in cash and benefits. If this person received a promotion to $15 an hour, they'll earn $5,451 more after taxes, but $8,336 less in benefits. That means that their income would decrease from $63,586 to $60,701 when taking this raise. If this person received a raise to $16 an hour their combined income and benefits would be about $50,000 a year which would result in an even larger drop.[122]

Perhaps the biggest and most dangerous issue is pensions to government employees. According to ITM Trading's Lynette Zang, only one state in the U.S. has a fully funded pension plan. Unfunded pension obligations rose from $292 billion to $1.9 trillion from 2007 to 2016. Furthermore almost 50% of pension asset allocation is held in stocks, almost 25% is held in derivatives and slightly more than 25% is held in bonds.[123] This is concerning considering the overvalued stock market and high risk bond market. Poor management of money by the government during the 2008 financial crisis resulted in a great loss of the money that was invested for pension plans. A lot of states are deeply in debt when it comes to their pension plans as a result. Despite the fact that many states are in massive debt, they still are offering raises to state workers to remain competitive, only making pension problems worse.

According to Statedatalab which looks at accounting numbers, California has $100.1 billion available in assets to pay $369.9 billion worth of bills. The outcome is a $269.8 billion dollar shortfall. To balance the budget, each tax payer in California would need to send the state $22,000. Currently the state has a $102.5 billion unfunded pension obligation.[124] The majority of this pension obligation is to the CalPERS—Public Employees Retirement Fund and the State Teachers' Retirement System. Currently, CalPERS has $436.7 billion in promised benefits and $298.1 billion in actual assets. This results in a $138.6 billion shortage, in which the state is responsible for 40%. The State Teachers' Retirement System has $302.8 billion in promised assets and $210.3 billion in actual assets which results in a $92.5 billion shortfall, in which the state is responsible for 36%.[125] Just these two plans result in $88 billion of unfunded pension benefits at the state level.

A huge problem with the pension system can be demonstrated with CalPERS. CalPERS—Public Employees Retirement Fund is the largest fund in the state of California and has a 7.15% discount rate. This effectively means that this fund guarantees a 7.15% return on investment per year. CalPERS is a management firm that manages the pensions and health benefits for nearly 2 million members. On a 3-year timescale the total net investment return has been 4.6%, on a 5-year timescale the return has been 8.8%, and on a 10-year timescale the return has amounted to 4.4%.[126] When evaluating this fund on a 3- and 10-year timescale, it is a far cry from the 7.15% guarantee.

The problem is that if the investments that CalPERS make produce a return lower than 7.15%, tax payers make up the difference. Since almost half the fund is in equities, if the stock market tanks, many people's livelihoods will be in jeopardy. Too many people have become dependent on this promised money. Does CalPERS have enough accountability for the risk they are taking with people's livelihoods? Some may argue that CalPERS still has time to turn a state like California around and has made progress through cutting benefits, but even so, they are still in a high risk situation. While states like California can still be saved, there are other states that have more serious problems. Places like Illinois are in so much financial trouble that it would require every person in the state to pay the government $50,800 to balance the budget.[127] According to Fox Business, Chicago would need 19 years' worth of taxes to balance their budget.[128]

While pensions are a huge concern, unfunded retiree health care and other nonpension, postemployment benefits for state and local employees are also a major issue. According to Statedatalab, New York alone has $110 billion of unfunded retiree health care liabilities.[129] One of the reasons this has gotten so out of hand is that for many years it was not required for states to report on retiree health care costs. Without any required disclosures, state and local governments could promise more health care benefits than they could possibly afford without being held accountable.

One of the big contributors to the pension and retiree health care crisis is Labor Unions. Many labor unions have become so powerful that they can influence an election and then ask for things that cannot possibly be fulfilled by government. Essentially the unions are trading votes for benefits. As people are living longer and investment growth is slowing, state governments are forced to pay out benefits longer, and go deeper into debt. Unfortunately, this is leading to higher taxes and fewer benefits for younger people in America. The only way that this will end is bankruptcy. In fact, according to Statedatalab.org five of the six most populous states in America received a D or F rating in debt. Only North Dakota, Wyoming and Alaska received an A.

Despite the severity of the pension and retiree health care crisis in the United States, it remains well hidden. One of the ways states hide this problem is by issuing municipal bonds. According to the Federal Reserve Bank of St. Louis, the liability for state and local governments' credit market instruments increased from $1.185 trillion in 2000 to nearly $3.08 trillion in 2018.[130] This is close to twice as much when adjusted for inflation. This would suggest increased risk, but despite this, bond yields remain near historic lows. Some still suggest that it is very unlikely that municipal bonds experience default, but in recent years Puerto Rico, Detroit, and Jefferson County, Alabama have all experienced municipal defaults. I would expect that many cities will join this list in the near future.

This chapter shows that many government programs are not sustainable financially in their current forms. In this country we ought to strive to get people off of welfare programs rather than incentivize people to join them. Excessive government pension plans and social security need to be slashed or eliminated. There is clearly no possible way that the U.S. can continue to make good on the false promises to older citizens. If the government wishes to continue to have these programs, they will need to raise taxes which will ultimately bring more people into poverty. The challenge in today's society is that so many people are dependent on the government and rely on goods and services more than they rely on themselves.

CHAPTER 10

The Danger of Fiat Money and the Banking System

One of the most important subjects that is completely ignored in the education system is an understanding of currency, fiat money and banking. Unfortunately this lack of understanding is creating risks for younger generations. A recent study by Bankrate claims:

"Three in ten millennials say cash is their favorite long-term investment, while each successive generation lays claims to stocks—a third of Gen Xers, 38% of baby boomers and 44% of the Silent Generation."[131]

Holding cash as an investment is a terrible idea and I aim to have everyone understand that by the end of the chapter, but to do this people need to have an understanding of the history of currency and fiat money.

When people think of currency they typically think of modern money like Dollars, Yen or Euros, but there have been many other types of currency. Throughout history different things have been used as currency, and it has evolved as time has gone on. For example, salt was once a highly valued resource used for currency in ancient times and was difficult to obtain due to laws that restricted its production. Cows, clam shells, rice, fish, barley, beads, and tea leaves have all served as currency during various times in history. However, as time wore on it became apparent that these currencies had problems. Some challenges were transportation, while others were whether the good would spoil, or how one would go about storing these items. Coinage became a great solution to this problem because metals are durable, portable and do not spoil. About 2,600 years ago, the Lydians, an ancient society based in what is modern-day Turkey, became the first western culture to introduce coins with set values.

Coins used in all ancient societies had a higher value than coins made today because they were often made from silver, bronze, gold, or some combination of those metals, rather than the copper, zinc and nickel used in many of today's coins. For many years coins were thought to be the best currency until the invention of printing.

Printing money was thought to be a great innovation in currency as it was significantly lighter and easier to trade than heavy metal coins. China would become the first nation to make paper bills during the Tang Dynasty (A.D. 618–907), but excessive production caused them to become nearly worthless and China eliminated paper money entirely in 1455.[132]

To combat the issue of excessive printing, when other nations began to adopt paper currency they began to index their currency to a resource. Most of these nations chose gold, and this would become known as the gold standard.

The gold standard meant that all of the paper money someone received could be exchanged for a certain amount of gold at the given nation's stockpile and that printing was limited based on how much gold a nation owned. Unfortunately all nations abandoned the gold standard in the last hundred years and we are starting to witness issues like that of China with overprinting. From 1998 to 2018 the currency in circulation in the United States rose from $492 billion to $1.67 trillion.[133] We have tripled the amount of money in circulation in just 20 years!

History has shown us that there have been hundreds of different fiat currencies, all of which on a long enough timespan have failed. Fiat currencies include any government-issued currency not backed by gold or silver, or by any physical commodity. Some of these currencies failed through hyperinflation, while others were destroyed by war, countries declaring independence, or monetary reformation. On a long enough timescale, the value of all fiat currencies decreases until it eventually drops to zero or is replaced. Researchers tend to argue as to the average time that a fiat currency lasts, but almost all agree that it is between 27–40 years.[134]

The oldest fiat currency in existence is the British pound Sterling which was founded in 1694. Many people tend to describe this as the most stable currency because of its long lifetime. However, over the years British money began to gradually contain less and less silver. Some might argue that silver was becoming a harder and harder to obtain resource, while others argue that governments just wanted to see how hard they could push people before they no longer trusted the currency. Prior to 1920, British silver coins contained high purity, 92.5% (Sterling) silver. From 1920 to 1946, British silver coins contained 50% silver. Since 1946 these coins contain no silver at all.[135] Keep in mind that when the British pound was first created over 300 years ago it was defined as twelve ounces of silver. Today it takes roughly thirteen British pounds to purchase just one ounce of silver. This means that the pound has about 1/156 the value that it once had and it has lost more than 99% of its value. The United States has experienced a similar process.

According to the Bureau of Labor Statistics' Consumer Price Index inflation calculator which has been used throughout this book, a dollar in January 1913, had the same buying power as $25.29 in January 2018. This shows about a 96% decline in the purchasing power of the dollar in the last 100 years.[136] The fact is, that the dollar is a terrible investment, because if you had $10,000 today and left it in a bank for ten years, you would have less purchasing power in ten years than you do today, this is due to the inflation being created by the continued printing of more and more money. But why can the U.S. just keep printing?

In 1973, a deal was struck between the United States and Saudi Arabia in which the U.S. would offer weapons and protection in exchange for the Saudis pricing all purchased oil into U.S. dollars. By 1975, all OPEC nations had agreed to price their own oil supplies exclusively in U.S. dollars in exchange for weapons and military protection. This would force all nations to convert their currencies into dollars and thus demand for U.S. dollars rose sharply. This was the birth of the petrodollar or in essence dollars for oil. This was a great strategy as nothing would have to back the dollar and the Federal Reserve could print as many dollars as they wanted in an attempt to control the economy.

If oil was not priced in dollars, the dollar would experience a significant crash in value. This is becoming a greater concern in today's market. Recently, there has been speculation that the Chinese will launch a gold-backed, Yuan-denominated oil futures contract with Russia. This means that oil purchases from Russia would be made strictly in the Chinese currency. If this "petroyuan" gains traction with other oil providers it may become the new backing for OPEC. It is very clear that an Alliance between China and Russia would pose a major risk to the future of the U.S. economy.

While the U.S. economy is very dependent on the petrodollar, it is also heavily dependent on foreign debt. The U.S. currently has over $6 trillion of foreign debt of which both China and Japan each own more than $1 trillion. So, what is keeping these countries from calling in this debt? When people from the U.S. buy Chinese goods, we pay dollars that they invest in America. If they were to take out their trillion dollars and invest it in Chinese money, it would bring the value of the dollar lower and more than double the value of Chinese money. But, if they do this, all the prices of their goods will become more expensive in America and thus American's will buy less. This will lead to a loss of jobs in China.

An important realization is that currency is ultimately based on trust and the way we have been printing money and operating our financial system is bending this trust to new levels. In the future it is probable that the financial and currency systems that govern America will fall apart, and this will be covered later in this book.

Section II: Five Keys to Success

The second section of this book explored the challenges associated with systems such as higher education, wages, finance and government programs. How might someone address these problems? Here are five ideas that people can use to improve their lives and address the challenges discussed in chapters 5 through 10.

1) **Have a Plan for Higher Education:** If you have kids or grandkids, sit down with them and talk about higher education. Research degrees and what the average pay is by major and how large loans will be to reach graduation. Create a plan and evaluate costs and benefits. Understand that not everyone is designed to go to college. If you are young and thinking about higher education, decide if a four-year university is right for you and realize that there are other options such as trade schools or community colleges. It's not impossible to be successful just because you chose not to go to an expensive university.

2) **Explore Alternative Sources of Skills and Employment:** Some people are great at working a 9 to 5 for their entire life and others struggle and would rather lead the way forward on their own projects and businesses. Are you an entrepreneur or a worker? Whether you are new to the workforce, a seasoned professional or run your own business, you can gain skills from sites like udemy, lydia.com, or skillshare. These sites offer specialized training at a fraction of the cost of a university. Many classes cost less than $100 dollars and can give you a huge advantage in advancement or differentiate you from other applicants. If you are willing to spend a little extra time, think about obtaining a certification or two. Certifications can really boost your potential earnings and command instant respect at a new job.

3) **Research and Vote:** Avoid getting information from large media companies when it comes to politics. They tend to have an agenda. Aim to get information from government agencies and use that information to evaluate things and vote. Vote for or against propositions or in general elections. Talk to your friends and family about your positions. Your vote matters.

4) **Contact Your State Elected Officials:** Reaching out to your states leaders can help promote change or help to clarify information. You can find out who your leaders are at the links provided below.
   Congressman/Congresswoman: https://www.house.gov/representatives
   Governor: https://www.usa.gov/state-governor
   Senator: https://www.senate.gov/general/contact_information/senators_cfm.cfm

5) **Use Your Social Media For Change:** Social media sites such as twitter can be extremely powerful. One tweet can gain traction and go viral, which can force the issue and your leaders to act. If there is something you do or don't like, speak up about it, but keep in mind that everyone, including potential employers, reads what you post online. Do not underestimate the power of social media. Even the president uses twitter.

WEALTH REDISTRIBUTION

CHAPTER 11

How the Wealthy and Powerful Prevent Economic Progress

Detroit was once considered to be one of the greatest manufacturing cities in the world. It was a vibrant place and the cornerstone for the American automotive industry. It gave birth to both the Ford Motor Company and the first cement highway. Detroit once bolstered a population of 1,850,000 in 1950; but by 2015, the population had dwindled to just 677,116.[137] According to Zillow, in December 2018, the median price of a house in Detroit was $41,500.[138] This was less than 20% of the $220,000 national average during the same time period.[139]

What happened to this once proud city? While changing technology and automation are often listed as some of the reasons why Detroit failed, the main issues were that Detroit had a single-industry-driven economy and that it had excessively high taxes. It can be argued that the economic collapse in Detroit was caused by the decisions of those who had power, and that too much power was in the hands of too few.

In modern society three groups of people control the power, the money, and ultimately the direction of the economy. One is called the 1%, which is comprised of extremely wealthy individuals. The second includes the central banks and large businesses. The third is the government. This chapter will be focusing on examples of wealth inequality, and how the incentives of these three groups are working against millennials, hindering economic progress, and hurting capitalism.

According to researchers at Reuters, as a group, the bottom 40% of Americans have a negative net worth.[140] The bottom 50% of American citizens own a smaller percentage of national wealth than almost all other countries in the world. While historically, a very small group of people have always controlled the vast amount of wealth in the U.S., the gap today is the largest that it has ever been. One example of this skewed wealth distribution can be witnessed in the ownership of land.

The top five landowning families in the United States own approximately 9 million acres of land which is equivalent to 14,062 square miles or about 10% larger than the size of Maryland. The top 25 landowning families own approximately 32,000 square miles or a chunk of land the size of South Carolina to put it in perspective.[141] [142] This is a harsh reality considering many Americans will never have the opportunity to own any land.

Since the 1970s we have experienced astronomical wealth gains by the top 1% of society, while many poor- and middle-class citizens continue to struggle. But who are these 1%? According to Pew Research, the top 10% of earners in the U.S. have 77.1% of the wealth and the top 1% have more than a third of all resources.[143] Most of the members of the 1% tend to be significantly older. According to the 2014 Census, the average net worth of a single person household with someone under the age of 35 is $4,166, in comparison to $118,700 of those aged 65 and older.[144] This shows that people over the age of 65 have over 25 times the net worth of those under the age of 35. Furthermore, the most recent agricultural census conducted in 2012, revealed that the average age of landlords who rented farmland was 66.5 years old, while only 18% were under 55.[145]

What made America so great for so long was the ability for young people to cultivate land and turn it into something valuable and useful. This has since faded, as young people are having a much harder time affording land, especially land that is located near coastal cities. As the wealth gap has become more pronounced between generations, we see all the land belonging to older people, yet these old people no longer have the energy to do anything productive with their land. Is it appropriate for older generations to let their land go to waste when there are so many millennials that would work hard to cultivate it? This hurts economic production as a whole.

In the last chapter it was shown that there are serious financial problems with government programs that help older citizens. Retiree health care for state workers, and social security, are becoming financially insolvent. Members of government and political parties know about this situation, but do their best to mask the problems and keep the money flowing. The issue is that older people are more likely to vote in elections and have more influence over these elections due to having more resources. This incentivizes government and political parties to meet the needs of these people before the needs of millennials. Ignoring the needs of millennials doesn't have as big a consequence on elections as imposing drastic cuts on benefits for the elderly.

Not surprisingly, many millennials are starting to question why there is such a lopsided and unfair wealth distribution in the United States. This has many steering away from our current governing economic system of capitalism in an effort to bring their standard of living closer to what their parents had at the same age. Even so, millennials are battling against the 1%, who have a high degree of influence, and took advantage of capitalism. The 1% are not incentivized to vote against our current system, considering they have used it to their advantage.

Capitalism is often represented as a highly efficient economic system that provides the best quality of life for consumers through **competition.** It is said that the choices of consumers help to dictate which companies are successful and which ones fail. People seek out the best quality products or the best available prices while companies vie for the business of these consumers and attempt to win them from competing firms. The problem with capitalism is that the incentive for a powerful company is to eliminate competition, with the goal to gain a larger customer base and to raise prices. On the other hand, citizens want competition so that they can get the best products and prices. Essentially, the system of capitalism works against itself. The main challenge capitalism is facing is that when massive companies take control of the market, they eliminate competition and make it more difficult for new companies to emerge. This leads to the point where only monopolies and oligopolies exist.

A monopoly occurs when a single entity has nearly complete control over an industry or service. A great example of this is De Beers which controls the diamond market or Monsanto (Bayer) which genetically modifies crops. In contrast to a monopoly, an oligopoly occurs when several companies control a market. An example of this might be AT&T, Verizon and T-Mobile who have strong control over the telecommunications industry. However, finding oligopolies isn't always transparent, and some oligopolies are more damaging and a higher risk to society than others.

When it comes to hidden oligopolies, a great example is witnessed in the case of nonalcoholic beverages. Walking into a grocery store, one is met with hundreds of drink options such as Fanta, Sprite, Powerade, Vitamin water, Mountain Dew and Gatorade. In this case there is an illusion of choice. In reality more than 60% of the nonalcoholic beverage industry is controlled by Coca-Cola and Pepsi. This is an example of a low-risk oligopoly because soft drinks aren't a necessary product or service that people require to live.

More dangerous examples of oligopolies can be witnessed in the financial industry and real estate industry. Many people have investments and retirement plans that are dependent on stocks, but most of the influence on Wall Street is held by hedge funds or massive financial corporations. There are approximately 10,000 to 15,000 active hedge funds that manage approximately $3 trillion. The top ten hedge funds are estimated to control close to $500 billion, or about a 1/6 of all the money in the system. The largest hedge fund is Bridgewater Associates, which oversees $150 billion in assets.[146] According to fortune.com the tenth largest company in the Fortune 500 is Bank of America, which is worth approximately $315 billion.[147] In this case, the Bridgewater Associates hedge fund controls resources that almost to almost half the value of a major bank. The reality is that the centralization of wealth around hedge fund managers can easily be used to topple some of the strongest companies in the world, or gain political power. It would only take the actions of a few hedge fund managers to create panic or buying frenzies in the stock market.

Another example of a dangerous oligopoly can be witnessed in real estate. After the subprime mortgage crisis of 2008, a company called Blackstone spent $10 billion dollars to buy and renovate about 50,000 properties, to be sold when the prices rose.[148] With this type of control over a market, this company could easily affect rent prices. I witnessed real estate oligopolies first hand during the time I lived in Fayetteville, Arkansas. A single company must have owned at least a third of all the apartments in the city. One has to question, at what point does the amount of control one small group has go too far?

In many ways it is the responsibility and actions of government to determine when a merger needs to be prevented and when a monopoly or oligopoly needs to be broken up. The government is supposed to ensure the success of capitalism by maintaining a marketplace with competition. But in an age where there is a consolidation of power among the elite and industries, does government act in the best interest of the people? In many cases big business has lobbyists to tell the government what to do, and not the other way around. This can result in the government creating monopolies and oligopolies, passing laws that go against the people, and looking the other way when there are corrupt business practices.

A great example of a government created monopoly is power providers in California. By introducing regulations that limit electric providers, there is no competition. Pacific Gas & Electric, Southern California Edison and San Diego Gas & Electric control the north, south and central region of the state and own almost all the power poles. This results in higher electricity costs for everyone in California.

In some cases pressure by big business is used to pass laws, even when citizens don't agree with these laws. For example, in 2011, a group of big businesses tried to pass SOPA (Stop Online Piracy Act). As a result, hundreds of websites banded together to try and stop the bill from passing. As I read hundreds of posts on online forums and other outlets, people vented about how bad the bill was and how they wanted it to fail. They equated it to a form of censorship and brutally opposed it. While most of these articles and the arguments they made lasted in my mind only several minutes, there was one post that left a lasting impression on me. One of the only people that wanted the bill to pass was a largely controversial internet figure simply known as Maddox. He wanted the bill to pass so that people would get so angry that they would actually do something about the greater problem behind it.

Maddox called the bill a "shitty piece of legislation put together by puppetmaster lobbyists and politician puppets who don't know IP addresses from their assholes." He stated that "We defeat SOPA today, only to face it again tomorrow. It's like trying to stop a cold by blowing your nose. It's time we go after the virus." By the virus, he was proposing to remove the very people that had suggested the bill. Lastly, in his article he said: "Check back in a few years, and there'll be another SOPA or Protect IP Act being squeezed down the lower intestinal tracts of congress."[149] In 2013, a new bill which was largely a rebranded version of SOPA called CISPA (Cyber Intelligence Sharing and Protection Act) passed, and did so largely without public knowledge. Maddox was completely right.

Of course, there are other situations where the government has acted against the best interest of the people to support big business. One such situation is bailouts. Many banks are subject to the "too big to fail" theory. This theory claims financial institutions, are so powerful and vital to the economy that they cannot be allowed to fail in any circumstance. Even in the case of gross negligence, governments use your tax dollars for bailouts to rescue financial companies that often just get away with just a simple slap on the wrist and some type of monetary fine. This can be viewed more like a bribe than a punishment.

According to a popular public interest journalism site called Propublica, the government has used taxpayer dollars to bail out 974 companies for a total of $625 billion. These companies range from government-sponsored enterprises like Fannie Mae and Freddie Mac to banks such as Bank of America and Citigroup.[150] Government bailouts were extremely popular after the 2007–2008 financial crisis. The government and taxpayers were forced to pay off the debts of irresponsible corporations that were facing bankruptcy such as JPMorgan Chase, Goldman Sachs, and Merrill Lynch.

The Urban Dictionary defines a bailout as "Broke people giving away their money so rich people don't go broke."[151] I find this definition to be disturbingly accurate. To think that there have been so many companies that required government bailouts is very unsettling. Our government is setting us on a dangerous path by allowing these bailouts to continue.

The power that central banks and large businesses have can also be used unethically and irresponsibly. Machiavelli once said that it is better to be feared than loved. Fear is a powerful emotion, and the fear of punishment helps to prevent immoral behavior and keep people in line. The problem with today's economy is the lack of fear and accountability that our large businesses and banks have.

Recently, Wells Fargo, which is one of the most powerful banks in America, created an estimated 3.5 million fraudulent savings and checking accounts on behalf of their clients without their consent.[152] Many of these accounts incurred charges and fees and it is without question that the actions Wells Fargo took are equivalent to downright thievery. Fearing the loss of their jobs and benefits, retail employees created fake accounts in order to meet unrealistic sales goals. Management created impossible sales goals in order to get bigger bonuses. It is amazing that in such a heavily regulated industry that this type of fraud was able to exist, but what really bothers me is that this had been happening since 2011 and had gone unnoticed for over 5 years.

As amazing as it sounds, it is unlikely that anyone will go to jail for this and Wells Fargo will most likely end up paying just $185 million or about 3% of their net quarterly income. This hardly seems like a punishment that will stop them from repeating this crime again in the future. Interestingly enough, this huge scandal received very little media coverage. What happened with Wells Fargo is very serious, and this isn't the only fraud in recent memory. Bernie Madoff, Enron, and Dynergy have all been subject of major scandals as well.

How can the incentives that work against common citizens and younger people be eliminated? How can we flip the script so that we can reestablish the American dream where anyone can be successful? While we may not be able to solve all of the wealth and power inequalities that have been mentioned in this chapter, the next few chapters will focus on possible solutions to increase the quality of life and help newer generations better compete in today's society.

CHAPTER 12

Socialism: Could This Solve Inequality?

One proposed way to solve wealth and power inequalities is through enacting socialism. It is thought that socialism would create free college, free health care, affordable housing provided by the government and redistribution of wealth to the middle class and poor by eliminating monopolies and oligopolies through government intervention. Some believe this will take America in a better direction than capitalism and praise it for the ability to reduce debt and level the playing field for everyone.

In recent years Socialism has been gaining traction, with most of its support coming from millennials and members of Generation Z. According to a January 2020 poll from Quinnipiac University, with the choice of twelve democratic candidates, 41% of people under the age of 35 said they would vote for Bernie Sanders who represents democratic socialism.[153]

In many ways socialism is turning into a movement rather than an economic system. This movement consists of members of younger generations who realize that they are more dependent on the success of their parents and grandparents than they are of themselves. It's getting difficult for millennials to continue to advocate for capitalism when they realize they have half of the purchasing power that their parents had at the same age (as was discussed in the second chapter). Shouldn't the prices of college degrees, medical care and housing be driven downward by competition in a capitalistic society?

Socialism is the concept that individuals should not have ownership of land, capital (money), or industry, but rather the whole community works together collectively. However, this can create some risks. Socialism can be viewed like a college group project. Sometimes one person does all the work and the other members of the group do nothing, but everyone gets the same grade. If this happens consistently, eventually that one person doing all the work gives up and stops trying. This is why Socialism poses risks to lowering economic production for people as a whole, as there simply isn't any motivation to create, and too many people are subject to mandated entitlements.

In its core form, socialism removes individual choice and allows government officials to decide how much a person should earn, which products and services are necessary for that person to live, and how much that person should have to pay for them. Essentially, it turns government into god. Redistribution of wealth relies upon force of government to take (steal) from the wealthy in order to give to the poor. Ben Shapiro claims that "it is immoral to steal from people even if you vote to steal from people." I would agree with this assessment; yet at the same time most of the people who have vast amounts of wealth inherited it and grew up privileged without having to work for it.

Despite the challenges that it faces, socialism is often branded as being the "most compassionate system" and the "ideal society." Implementing it in America would (in theory) eliminate mortgages, medical debt, and college loans which are three of the largest sources of debt in the country. Education would be available to those who chose it, not just the rich, and excessive debt would no longer hold younger people hostage.

When evaluating styles of government, it is important to understand that no country is completely socialistic and no country is completely capitalistic. Almost all countries have a blending of principles from both capitalism and socialism. Dozens of countries have adopted or tried to adopt different versions of Socialism in the past. North Korea, India, China, Cuba, and Venezuela represent traditional socialism where government controls virtually everything about a person's life. Sweden, Norway, and Denmark represent a style of government that is often referred to as a social democracy but can also be referred to as to the Nordic Model, Nordic Social Democracy, or Nordic Capitalism. In this model, government and government officials DO NOT decide how much a person should earn, but rather this is determined by free market capitalism. So, it can be argued in some people's eyes that the Nordic Model is not true socialism.

When criticizing socialism, people often use Venezuela and Cuba as examples. In the 1950s and 60s Venezuela experienced amazing wealth, in fact it was the 4th largest wealth producer in terms of GDP per capita in 1950. However, challenges with oil prices and poor leadership led a prosperous country into socialism. Today in Venezuela, people are starving, there are food riots, and medicines are almost nonexistent. The IMF predicts that hyper-inflation in Venezuela will exceed 1.37 million percent this year.[154] In the case of Cuba, Castro took over thousands of businesses and outlawed private enterprise. While today Cuba has free health care, many doctors and engineers who are employed by the state work in their free time as taxi drivers or servers because these positions actually pay more.

When people argue for socialism they often do so citing the Nordic Model. Nordic Social Democracy experiences low levels of corruption and citizens are given access to socialist programs such as free education and universal health care programs paid for by the government. At the same time, a high percentage of workers belong to labor unions, there are excellent worker protection rights, and there is no need for minimum wage laws. In addition, all five of the Nordic countries that use democratic socialism ranked in the Top 10 on the World Happiness Report, which is an annual publication of the United Nations.

However, the thing most people fail to realize about the Nordic model is that these countries rely on the extremely high taxes to support their programs. For example, the highest personal income tax rate is 51.27% in Sweden, while in the U.S. it is only 37%.[155] At the same time these Nordic countries rely on the U.S. to supplement their defense as they have very little military. This allows Sweden, Norway, and Denmark to spend more on social programs and gives the illusion that this version of socialism can work anywhere when in fact it probably wouldn't.

The U.S. spends $647 billion a year on military while Norway spends $7 billion, Sweden spends $6.2 billion and Denmark spends $4.4 billion.[156] The U.S. spends about 35 times more on military than these three socialistic countries combined. Unlike Scandinavian countries, the United States is almost forced to have a huge military because of the petrodollar. Essentially the U.S. trades guns for OPEC to price oil in U.S. dollars. This makes the U.S. dollar strong because all other nations need to convert their currency into dollars to purchase oil.

The reality is that enacting some form of socialism will most likely fail in America. The traditional model where government uses force to take (steal) from the wealthy in order to give to the poor has never worked. The Nordic model would require a small military which goes against the incentives of the U.S. and would most likely fail on a financial level. At the same time, the failure of socialism might lead to hyperinflation which could be a better way to solve wealth and power inequalities.

CHAPTER 13

Hyperinflation and Debt Forgiveness

Another proposed way to solve wealth and power inequalities is through debt forgiveness or hyperinflation. Both people and government are experiencing record amounts of debt at current time. The U.S. government had $22.7 trillion of debt as of September 2019, and its debt has more than doubled since 2008.[157] As stated in the second chapter, Americans have $13.21 trillion of household debt as of 2018. Lowering the debt burden held by younger generations would reduce their overhead, which would free up more cash. This would result in an increased standard of living and would possibly lead to more entrepreneurship due to less financial constraints.

Debt forgiveness is an unlikely scenario, as it is highly costly to the government, and the government already has a substantial amount of debt. However, there are several examples of where governments bailed out citizens by forgiving their debt.

One of the first examples of debt being absolved by the government appeared more than 3,500 years ago in Mesopotamia. The 48th provision of the Code of Hammurabi was one of the first legal codes for debt forgiveness and stated that:

"If any one owe a debt for a loan, and a storm prostrates the grain, or the harvest fail, or the grain does not growth for lack of water, in that year he need not give his creditor any grain, he washes his debt-tablet in water and pays no rent for this year."

This law was largely written because of the threat of drought, and helped to protect farmers.

Another example of debt forgiveness happened recently in the United States. In 2015, The U.S. Education Department discovered that Corinthian College misrepresented job placement data, altered grades and provided false attendance records. They decided to fine the college $30 million and the school responded by shutting down. This left students with worthless degrees, nontransferable credit and big loans. The government decided to offer these former students debt forgiveness and it is estimated that the cost to the government and tax payers could hit $3.5 billion.

A far more likely situation to occur in the United States is hyperinflation. The United States and world for that matter are at a much higher risk for hyperinflation today due to the fact that there is no gold standard and nations are printing new fiat currency recklessly. America's debt is also growing faster than its economy which is growing at roughly 2.4% as of 2019.[158] This means that at the current rate of debt growth, the U.S. will eventually not be able to pay its debts. This combined with high wealth imbalances between the wealthy and poor and many people living outside of their means is creating a scenario where it is quite possible that the dollar will completely fail, or be replaced with an entirely new currency.

Hyperinflation is defined as when inflation exceeds 50% per month and lasts for at least 30 consecutive days. For example if a loaf of bread costs $4 one month and then costs $6 the next month you could refer to this 50% increase as hyperinflation. However hyperinflation affects all goods, not just a single one.

According to the Hanke-Krus-Hyperinflation-table, there have been 58 instances of hyperinflation over the last 100 years. Nations such as France, China, Greece, and Russia are just a few of the countries that made the list. However the severity of their hyperinflation has varied widely. On the low end is Taiwan which experienced hyper-inflation of about 51% in February 1947, and on the high end was Hungary in August 1945 which experienced hyperinflation that was so severe, that it was estimated that prices would double every 15 hours.[159] Imagine needing to bring a wheelbarrow loaded with paper money to buy a pair of socks.

Hyperinflation can be terrifying; in some cases the paper money of a government loses value so quickly that it is no longer worth working. Why should you work at a job when several days later you receive a paycheck that is nearly worthless? In the short term the effects of hyperinflation can be dangerous and unsettling, but in the longer term it could be a great solution to fix the U.S. economy.

One example where hyperinflation ended up helping to fix debt can be seen in early 20th century Germany. From 1921 to 1924, the German mark suffered hyperinflation. To pay for the costs of World War I, Germany removed itself from the gold standard. Rather than using taxes to pay for the war, German Emperor Wilhelm II decided to fund the war entirely by borrowing. It sounded like a great idea, but when Germany lost the war, the government was now saddled with a massive unaffordable war debt. In 1917, it took approximately 5.53 Reichsmarks (paper marks) to buy $1 and by December 1923, it took approximately 3.43 billion Reichsmarks.[160] Let that sink in for a second.

Ultimately Germany would eliminate the mark and replace it by introducing the Rentenmark ("mortgage mark"), backed by bonds indexed to the market price of gold. Rentenmarks were not redeemable in gold but only indexed to the gold bonds. This was in many ways a catastrophe, but the one thing that was good about this was that due to hyperinflation, all the debts were essentially absolved. In other words, because the money crashed in price, the existing debt disinte-grated in value so much that everyone could easily afford to pay off all their debts.

Venezuela is one of the two countries experiencing hyper-inflation currently. They are trying to replace a broken currency like early 1900's Germany; however they are handling the situation differently. Instead of making an effort to go back to some type of gold standard, they are attempting to be the first country on an entirely digital currency. In February 2018, the government of Venezuela launched the Petro also known as the Petromoneda which is a cryptocurrency said to be backed by the country's oil and mineral reserves. Digital currencies such as Bitcoin have gained a lot of traction in recent years because they eliminate some of the biggest problems in financial systems and central banks, but it remains to be determined if a digital standard will work in modern economies. Digital currencies will be evaluated in a later chapter.

Considering the likelihood of a currency collapse in the United States, investing in some precious metals or cryptocurrency would most likely be an excellent idea for millennials. It is very possible that one day in the near future people will trade gold, silver or some type of digital currency for houses and no longer use dollars. The next two chapters will explore how this might work.

CHAPTER 14

A Return to Precious Metals

Gold and silver are universal; they are accepted across all countries and all cultures. You can always convert gold and silver into any good, service, or currency. Precious metals are tangible assets that you can hold in your hand. There is only a finite amount of these metals in existence, and one day there will be no more left to mine. Currently, there is no way to create gold or silver out of nothing in some special lab. The amount of protection precious metals offers you as a storage of wealth is unparalleled. With the risk of a financial collapse due to debt, I believe every millennial should have at least some silver and gold.

Precious metals also have other significant uses. The digital age has brought us many electronics and a lot of these electronics require gold and silver in order to produce. In an age where these metals have a limited supply and are being burned up for other purposes, it is unquestioned that in the future they will gain a significant amount of value.

Silver has heavy industrial demand and roughly a third of it is used in electronics as a conductor or a contact in electrical switches. Silver is used in computers, keyboards, televisions, batteries, cell phones, calculators, cameras, watches, clocks, and microwave ovens. Silver is also used in coins, medals, jewelry, silverware, photography and even solar panels. Considering the wide range of applications, silver will always have value.

Gold is unique as it conducts electricity and does not tarnish. It is used in most electronic devices, including computers and cell phones. Gold contained in connectors, switches and relay contacts allows electronic based devices to remain free of corrosion. Gold can also be used in jewelry, aerospace and the medical world.

There are also several other precious metals of great value, such as palladium and platinum. The main use of palladium and platinum is in catalytic converters in car exhaust systems. A catalytic converter helps to convert the toxic substances in engine exhaust into inert or less toxic substances. Palladium can also be used as a multilayer ceramic capacitor which is an important part used in modern electronics such as cellphones and laptops.

Most professionals look at precious metals as a storage of value and not an investment. As a storage of value precious metals will always be worth something. If we experience hyperinflation it is most likely that the value of things like gold and silver will inflate as well, meaning you will never lose purchasing power.

Nearing the release of this book, COVID-19 is starting to impact America. Historic job losses combined with economic instability is putting pressure on all governments to spend trillions of dollars. This makes hyperinflation highly possible and metals a must-have investment that is far safer than just holding dollars. Your cash could be worthless in several months, but your silver and gold will always be worth something.

When it comes to viewing precious metals as an investment, I disagree with the financial professionals who believe that precious metals are not an investment. I find that mathematically they are highly undervalued. Unlike most other markets, the silver market is quite small. In 1979, the Hunt Brothers who were the sons of a Texas oil billionaire, attempted to gain a complete monopoly over the silver market. Silver would increase in price from $6 in 1979 to

$50 in January 1980.[161] While the brothers ultimately failed, it was estimated at one point in time that they owned approximately 1/3 of all the silver in existence. People who were fortunate enough to buy when the price was at the bottom and sell when the profits were at the top would have made more than seven times their investment.

The point that I am trying to make is that as the demand goes higher for precious metals their purchasing power will also increase. In a crisis, I would expect that much of the older generation will be the people who will push the price of precious metals higher; due to the fact that they are not as comfortable with modern technology as the younger generations.

The gold to silver ratio is how many ounces of silver it takes to buy one ounce of gold. In ancient times from 1,000 B.C to the 1800s the gold-to-silver ratio was in most parts of the world between 10–15 to 1. Alexander the Great set the relationship of gold to silver at 10 to 1 and in 1792, Congress under President George Washington fixed the U.S. gold-to-silver ratio at 15 to 1. In 1889 the ratio reached 20 to 1 and by 1900 it was 37 to 1.[162] This ratio would stay close to the 1900 level over the next 30 years until 1930 when it shot to 63 to 1.[163] As of 2019, the gold to silver ratio is approximately 75 to 1. This number makes little sense considering the historical cumulative gold-to-silver production ratio is 10.7 to 1.

According to GFMS, Thomson Reuters and the Silver Institute, 885.8 million ounces of silver was mined in 2016, equivalent to approximately 25,112 Metric Tons. According to Statista 3,100 metric tons of gold was mined in 2016. This shows that roughly 8.1 ounces of silver is being mined for every 1 ounce of gold. From the years 2000 to 2015 we have experienced twelve years of deficit in the silver market and four years of surplus. In the last ten years we have had a deficit of more than 600 million ounces of silver, which is equivalent to almost one complete year of global mining production.[164]

There is virtually no correlation between the price of silver and physical surpluses and deficits over the last sixteen years, which shows that the paper price of silver does not actually represent its true demand. In other words, the price of silver is artificially low. It is mathematically impossible that the gold-to-silver ratio stays at 75 to 1 with the lack of production, continued deficits, and increasing demand. Based on this information it is most likely that the price of silver will reach a ratio of between 10 and 20 ounces to one ounce of gold making the price of silver roughly $60-$125 per ounce within the next few years.

When it comes to currency, in the short term it is possible for us to return to a gold standard and remove ourselves from the petro-dollar. This might happen when there is a severe stock market crash, or if money is printed out of control and we experience hyperinflation. However it is highly unlikely that gold or silver will act as direct currency. One challenge is that gold and silver are difficult to protect and require a safe. Another issue is that if you had a large bar of silver or gold how could you cut part of it off and use it to pay for something. This would require scales and a lot of extra work for merchants. In today's age, silver and gold may be the safest and longest lasting storage of value, but they are bulky and difficult to trade in comparison to paper money or cryptocurrency.

Moving forward, one of two things is likely to happen. Either there will be a push to go back to the gold standard form of banking where the printing of our money is based on the resources we own or we will move towards some form of a cashless society. Exciting new technologies are developing currently and offer many advantages over traditional currencies. Many young people are flocking to online digital currency such as Bitcoin. The next chapter will focus on what a Bitcoin is, why people are excited about it, and how it might just change everything.

CHAPTER 15

Bitcoin: the Solution to our Problems?

Since the start of writing this book, Bitcoin has gone from a relatively obscure concept to a nationally recognized currency traded on Wall Street. This chapter has been rewritten about half a dozen times. During the first revision, a single Bitcoin cost about $1,700. After being released on Wall Street at the end of 2017, Bitcoin experienced a meteoric rise to nearly $20,000 before falling off a cliff. Some have called it digital gold and some fear its high volatility. It does, however, offer a unique storage of value. Bitcoin was the first modern cryptocurrency and is the most publicized. There are actually over 2,000 other cryptocurrencies with varying uses and goals. This chapter will mainly focus on Bitcoin, but will also make mention of Ethereum and Bitcoin Cash which are other cryptocurrencies that offer unique solutions to both economic and technological problems.

Bitcoin has been discussed in Netflix documentaries, YouTube videos, and the mainstream media much more than the other cryptocurrencies. Some famous people in the technology industry have been interviewed about it including Microsoft's Bill Gates, inventor Elon Musk, cyber security expert John McAfee, and Virgin Galactic founder Richard Branson. In an interview with Bloomberg, Bill Gates said:

"Bitcoin is exciting because it shows how cheap it can be. Bitcoin is better than currency in that you don't have to be physically in the same place and, of course, for large transactions, currency can get pretty inconvenient."[165]

John McAfee posted on twitter that Bitcoin would hit one million by 2020 and that he would "eat his own dick if he's wrong about Bitcoin."[166]

Some could argue that this type of publicity is overinflating the price, but it is the strength of the community and the trust within that community that will determine the value, not necessarily whether the underlying asset is the best or not. Despite all of the recent attention, many people have a very limited knowledge as to what cryptocurrency is and how it works. Few understand what is so special about Bitcoin and why it was created in the first place. Many people are left scratching their heads as to how cryptocurrency went from nothing to having a market capitalization of several hundred billion dollars. To understand Bitcoin and cryptocurrency, you need to understand how and why it was started.

In November 2008, a paper was posted to a cryptography mailing list under the name Satoshi Nakamoto titled Bitcoin: A Peer-to-Peer Electronic Cash System. Bitcoin was originally built in response to the 2007 financial crisis and aimed to thwart future collapses. It was described as "a system for electronic transactions without relying on trust." Bitcoin has no physical form and is entirely digital. It is bought online mainly through the use of cryptocurrency exchanges and then stored on digital wallets which can be on someone's computer, cellphone or cold storage wallet device. Like our current paper currency, there is no gold- or silver-based backing to this online currency.

The first few years of Bitcoin were rocky. In 2011, a black market system and the first modern darknet market called the Silk Road used Bitcoins anonymity on a hidden part of the internet for buying and selling illegal drugs. Silk Road allowed people to buy almost anything anonymously and Bitcoin was the perfect currency to keep these transactions hidden from sight. The site was eventually shut down by the FBI, but gave Bitcoin a bad reputation in the process.

Another huge hurdle was seeing the world's largest Bitcoin exchange go bankrupt. Launched in July 2010, Mt. Gox was a Bitcoin exchange that by 2014 was estimated to handle over 70% of the world's Bitcoin transactions. In 2014, Mt. Gox announced that approximately 850,000 Bitcoins belonging to customers and the company were missing and likely stolen. Soon after this announcement Mt. Gox went bankrupt, and most of the missing Bitcoins were never to be seen again.

Today, new technology such as cold storage wallets, and more regulations around cryptocurrency exchanges have led to much safer conditions and allowed Bitcoin and other cryptocurrencies to thrive. After existing for about ten years, Bitcoin is showing signs of a maturing market and isn't going to be going away anytime soon. Now, many people reading this are going to ask the question, why exactly would I want a Bitcoin and what makes it special or better than fiat currency such as dollars? After all, it would seem most of the information I have provided shows it in a somewhat negative light.

Bitcoin's greatest value lies with the technology system it introduced called the blockchain. The blockchain allows more efficient and safer transactions than our current banking process and also has the ability to solve two of the biggest problems that have been talked about in most of this book. A widespread adoption of Bitcoin or other cryptocurrency would hopefully force people to live within their means rather than continue to borrow absurd amounts of money. With no or less debt, prices of things like cars and houses would be pushed lower as fewer people would be able to afford them. Bitcoin also solves the issues associated with endless printing of fiat currency. No longer would you need to worry about hyperinflation or mismanagement of a currency that would cause it to be worthless in the future. But how exactly does Bitcoin do this?

Firstly, Bitcoin transactions cannot be reversed, do not carry personal information, and are all recorded on the blockchain. This protects merchants and people using it from potential losses from fraud. Bitcoin is a "push" system, while our current banking system is built around a "pull" model. If you went to buy a service and give the merchant your debit card or credit card, they will get your information and pull the money. One of the issues with this, is if you buy a $10 dollar item and the merchant accidently adds an extra zero, which would mean you would be charged $100 instead of $10. Bitcoin acts more like cash, rather than a debit or credit card. You send the person the amount; they don't pull it from you. This drastically reduces errors.

The blockchain system that Bitcoin runs on creates a public ledger and then proceeds to add additional information to that ledger after every transaction takes place. Imagine this as a giant spreadsheet that keeps track of every place that your money has been since it was created. When people chose to buy something with Bitcoin, their transactions are lumped into clumps of other transactions that are called blocks, these blocks are then placed in order on the ledger, hence the word blockchain. Blocks are added to the ledger by "Bitcoin miners" or as I like to call them, nerds with really powerful computers. These miners then receive a small tip or transaction fee for adding blocks to the ledger. In other words, someone with a powerful computer uses their computing power to support the Bitcoin network and validate your transaction for a very small financial incentive. In addition, these miners release a small amount of currency into existence if their computer is able to solve the math problem the fastest.

Since the blockchain is self-sustaining, there is no need for any organizations, companies or governing authority to regulate or distribute Bitcoin. This is what is referred to as decentralized. Decentralization helps to eliminate control or manipulation where special interests may have an impact on currency. Unlike fiat currency, the supply of Bitcoin is limited. Currently there are just over 16 million Bitcoins in existence. This number of Bitcoins will reach a maximum of 21 million when the last one is mined in 2140. In a previous chapter I talked a lot about trust and how it is vital to a currency. Bitcoin offers a major advantage in this area because it will never be subject to the endless printing that has become common with fiat currency.

Bitcoin is immune to inflation. As we continue to constantly produce more and more paper money, the value of that money diminishes. In a place like the United States, we experience an inflation rate of 2.3% for the year ending February 2020, meaning that the costs of goods and services tend to get about 2.3% more expensive each year due to more money in circulation. We are heavily reliant on the Federal Reserve and our government when it comes to both printing and managing our money. Like many other nations, the U.S. is at risk of experiencing hyperinflation within the next few years. Hyperinflation is extremely rapid or out of control inflation that is often caused by the overprinting or mismanagement of money. Over the last 25 years many countries have experienced hyperinflation such as Zimbabwe, Argentina, Brazil, Mexico, Poland, and Russia to name a few.

As of writing this book, $1 can be traded for €.86 and €1 can be traded for 0.00019 Bitcoins. Now in the event of hyperinflation, in six months $1 might only be worth €.50 and in a year perhaps it's only worth €.20. However, even if the dollar is only worth €.20, €1 is still worth 0.00019 Bitcoins. In other words, you have lost value if you held dollars; you didn't if you had Bitcoins. This is why many people from places like Zimbabwe have adopted Bitcoin as it protects them from the type of currency instability and hyperinflation that their nation is currently experiencing.

Unlike using PayPal or a bank that charges you money to use its technology, Bitcoin has extremely low fees because you only need to pay your miner a small tip. Suppose you want to send $100 to someone out of country. Bank of America would charge you $45 to send that money via an outbound international wire service, while a Bitcoin transaction would be significantly cheaper.[167] This is not even taking into account other hidden bank transfer fees. However, despite the fact that many cryptocurrencies have very low fees in transactions, many people buy them through online exchanges that charge a fee for purchasing. Most of the exchanges have fees that range from 1.5% to 4%. So, while transactions have little to no cost, obtaining cryptocurrency can offset this.

Bitcoin can be broken into 8 decimal places allowing it to be used on all transactions no matter how cheap or expensive. Exchanges allow the purchase of any amount of Bitcoin you want. In the case of the stock market, millennials generally cannot afford to buy a share of an expensive stock such as Apple, so why not buy a fractional share ownership of Bitcoin?

Bitcoin also has some other major advantages over credit cards. One such advantage is that you do not need to spend five minutes typing in your card information in order to pay for something. Using our current system, your average credit or debit card transaction goes through three stages. These three stages are Authorization, Authentication, and Clearing & Settlement. This tends to be a 16-step verification process that involves the cardholder, merchant, acquirer, credit card network, and issuing bank. They also carry per-swipe fees of about 2.35% plus $0.15.[168]

Bitcoin doesn't need a 16-step verification process, needs only one other party (the miner), and in most cases a transaction takes a few seconds to start and the other person will receive payment within several minutes.

So, to do a quick recap, Bitcoin is less prone to fraud, immune to inflation and cheaper to send than our current system using credit cards or banks. On top of all this, you are in control of your money and don't have to deal with banks.

I recently needed to buy a product from a manufacturer in France. I placed the order, but when I tried to pay with my debit card the transaction was denied, and on top of that my bank froze my account "suspecting fraudulent activity." I called the bank telling them to let the transaction through, and of course they still didn't. I found out that the company I was buying from accepted Bitcoin, and then proceeded to buy the product I needed with Bitcoin. It was far easier than using my debit card, and far less problematic.

Although less than 1% of businesses worldwide accept Bitcoin as a form of payment, there are a few powerful companies that do accept it. Currently: Microsoft, Tigerdirect, Dell, Tesla, Square, Kmart, Sears, and Dish Network all accept Bitcoin. You can even buy gold or silver using Bitcoin through JM Bullion or APMEX. Bitcoin has built a strong and powerful network of users and followers. Last year Japan and Russia recognized Bitcoin as a legal form of payment which has brought a lot of excitement and new buyers into Bitcoin. This was seen as a major victory for crypto-currencies in general.

People, businesses and governments act in what is in their best interest. The surge in Bitcoin and other cryptocurrencies has led to some panic within the finance and banking industry. If people no longer needed the services of credit cards and banks, these businesses would be forced to either evolve or die. This is one of the major motivating factors for banks, the finance industry, and credit cards to get involved with this process, and either join a cryptocurrency, or try and introduce their own payment system. There is quite a bit of motivation to move to a cashless society.

In July 2017, Visa began offering restaurants and food vendors across the U.S. rewards of up to $10,000 for upgrades to technology that encourage electronic payment, on the condition that they stop accepting physical cash.[169] In an age of technological innovation where most things have gradually become computerized and digital, it would make sense that currency would become digital as well. Roughly 2 billion people do not have access to a physical bank and about 1 billion of these people have access to a cellphone. Having access to more customers means more profits, and this is a motivating factor for big banks and credit cards. A cashless society also allows credit companies and banking more control over money and transactions than our current credit system.

Another entity that can benefit from a cashless society is the U.S. government. One challenge that the U.S. currently faces is that pennies cost about 1.5¢ to produce and are only worth 1¢. In other words, they cost more to manufacturer than they are worth. In May 2012, Canada decided to discontinue their penny which will save their taxpayers an estimated $11 million each year.[170] At what point, though, do the nickel, dime and quarter become removed as well? If the government removed us from the physical banking system of coinage that we have, they would save millions of dollars.

Arguably the strongest financial entity in the world is the International Monetary Fund. The IMF is an organization of 189 countries, working to foster global monetary cooperation, secure financial stability, facilitate international trade, promote high employment and sustainable economic growth, and reduce poverty around the world.[171] In the event of a financial crisis, the IMF has the ability to act as a central bank and print dollars. Christine Lagarde who was the head of the International Monetary Fund until recently spoke at the Singapore Fintech Festival on November 13, 2018. In her speech she stated:

"I believe we should consider the possibility to issue digital currency. With appropriate design, there may be a role for the state to actually supply money to the digital economy."[172]

This helps to cement the idea of a cashless society and an age where cryptocurrency is used to pay for everything.

All of the big credit cards have become interested in cryptocurrency. In 2017 Visa launched the Monero Debit Card which uses the cryptocurrency known as Monero to pay for things. Mastercard joined the Ethereum Enterprise Alliance and will most likely attempt to integrate their payment systems with the second largest cryptocurrency known as Ethereum. American Express began supporting a Bitcoin digital wallet application for smartphones called Abra. Cryptocurrency has the potential to greatly benefit credit cards, and more companies are taking notice with each passing day.

However, despite all of the advantages and the motivation to use cryptocurrency, it is not without critics. Many of the most vocal opponents against it tend to have one of three things in common. Either they have ties to big banks, have special interests in it failing, or are uncomfortable because they don't understand the new technology. Some big names that oppose cryptocurrency include: finance and debt specialist, Dave Ramsey; American Nobel Laureate, Robert Shiller; CEO of JPMorgan, Jamie Dimon; Mad Money host, Jim Cramer; and investor, Warren Buffet. These people tend to have rather poor arguments as to why they believe cryptocurrency will fail. Many of these people criticize cryptocurrencies like Bitcoin as being a massive bubble or a fraud and compare it to Tulip-Mania. Tulip-Mania was a period between 1636 and 1637 when Dutch people were paying more than 10 times their annual income for a single tulip bulb. Personally, I find this to be a rather ridiculous comparison.

Nevertheless, the cryptocurrency movement is not without problems and faces major challenges both internally and externally. When it comes to internal challenges pertaining to the technology of cryptocurrency, there are three major issues. The first issue is decentralization. While decentralization offers less corruption, more efficiency and less manipulation to a currency, there are also those who argue that it leads to indecision and fracturing of communities. One such example of this is Bitcoin vs. Bitcoin Cash. When Bitcoin transactions started to get slower and more expensive due to a huge explosion of users, a group of Bitcoin miners split off and created their own version of Bitcoin called Bitcoin Cash. Bitcoin Cash has more development teams and uses variable block sizes in the blockchain to reduce transaction costs. However, this is problematic because it fractures the community, and divides them. If I were a company accepting Bitcoin and then it crashes and is replaced by Bitcoin Cash, I might lose interest in cryptocurrency altogether.

The second internal challenge that cryptocurrency faces is scalability. As more people use cryptocurrency, the transactions tend to get slower and more expensive. If widespread adoption and acceptance is to occur for Bitcoin or Ethereum, their networks need to be able to handle significantly higher volumes of transactions. The future success of cryptocurrency is largely dependent on Amazon or Ebay accepting it as a valid payment method. While being able to process several transactions per second is great, it pales to the several hundred transactions per second that major ecommerce sites receive. Currently, Bitcoin is working on the "Lightening Network" and Ethereum is working on the "Raiden Network" to try and solve this problem.

The third major internal issue with Bitcoin is the severe ownership imbalance. It is estimated that only 927 people own half of all Bitcoins.[173] This means that the actions of just a single person can cause a very significant movement in price. While this is a valid argument, just eight super-rich men hold the same amount of wealth as the poorest half of the world's population. This means that Bitcoin is actually less unbalanced than our current system. Recently, Rothschild & Co which is one of the most powerful groups of people in the world filed a $210,000 Bitcoin purchase through A Bitcoin Investment Fund. The question now becomes, are Bitcoin and the other major cryptocurrencies just a major oligopoly where only a few people control everything?

Cryptocurrency also has three major external challenges. These three threats are government regulation, exchange/wallet safety, and large banks/corporations. Some governments have banned or put a stop on Bitcoin. Bolivia, Kyrgyzstan, Bangladesh, Nepal and Vietnam have all made Bitcoin completely illegal. Recently, larger and more valuable players in the cryptocurrency market such as India, China, and South Korea have all been threatening to ban or severely regulate cryptocurrency. Many of these countries have imposed extremely high taxes on cryptocurrency in an attempt to try and strangle it. Even the United States has gotten into the taxation of cryptocurrency, and recently demanded that the largest U.S. exchange Coinbase hand over records of all their users.

Governments realized that they could not regulate cryptocurrency directly, and have instead turned their sights to the exchanges themselves, making it harder or more expensive to buy crypto-currency. Despite this, it's extremely unlikely that Bitcoin will ever be banned in the United States. In 2014, Janet Yellen the Chair of the Board of Governors of the Federal Reserve System declared that Bitcoin was a "Payment innovation taking place entirely outside the banking industry" and "the federal reserve does not have authority to supervise or regulate Bitcoin in any way because there is no central issuer or network operator to regulate."[174]

The second major challenge Bitcoin faces is exchange/wallet safety. In the past, exchanges used to buy Bitcoin have gone bankrupt, out of business, or removed service from demographic areas. This would mean that all the cryptocurrency you have stored on the exchange would disappear. In fact, over 30 exchanges have been closed for one or another reason. This happened in 2014 when Mt. Gox went bankrupt. In 2017, Bitfinex removed its services from its U.S.-based customers because of its disagreement with new U.S. SEC regulations. As more news comes out about closing exchanges and hackers that have stolen cryptocurrency, it leads to questions as to how safe your cryptocurrency really is. Can you be hacked? Can you lose everything? The reality is that cryptocurrency is safe if you set up the appropriate safety precautions. The problem is that many people are not very well educated as to what these precautions entail. The best way to keep your digital wallet safe is through a two-factor authentication system, or by using a cold storage wallet in which you take your crypocurrency offline.

In the case of leaving your currency online, you should enable two-factor authentication with Google authenticator and require a password. Google authenticator is a free application you can install on your smartphone. It has a code that changes every 30 seconds. In this case it would require someone to have access to your physical phone, exchange password and email to access your digital wallet. This method is unhackable, but you need to keep close tabs on your phone.

The second option is to use a cold storage wallet. Cold storage wallets allow you to take your cryptocurrency offline and store it in an extremely secure manner that looks like a small flashdrive. These cold storage devices have phrases that you can use to recover your cryptocurrency should anything happen. Currently there are two main companies that offer cold storage wallets. One is called Ledger and the other is called Trezor. For several hundred dollars you can purchase one of these digital safes that you should keep in a safe place in your house.

The third major issue facing cryptocurrency is large businesses that are trying to stop it. In early 2018, Chase, Bank of America, and Citi all banned the purchase of Bitcoin and other cryptocurrencies using credit. While Bitcoin could benefit these banks, many are increasingly cautious. This gives rise to several important questions. Was there collusion between these banks, and was this legal for them to do? Is it appropriate that banks refuse to allow you to purchase something using credit?

Another challenge coming from big business is from Facebook and Google. Both of these companies have banned all advertisements for cryptocurrency. This is partially because they argue that ICOs or Initial Coin Offerings are unsafe and scam-like. There are also people who argue that these companies control the world and want cryptocurrency to fail so that they maintain the power. It has become quite scary how much influence and power some companies have in America. This could be a strong threat for a future with the desire for change.

Despite the challenges that Bitcoin and the cryptocurrency market faces, there are many young people, including myself, who believe that it will become widely accepted as the new global standard for money. Bitcoin offers a new beginning for a generation that is facing desperation and poverty. As I stated earlier in this book, people over the age of 50 have about 77% of the wealth. Bitcoin offers a unique way for wealth distribution without the need for something as extreme as socialism. Many of the older people in America lack the understanding of how to acquire Bitcoin, or are content to just not own it. Much as many older people still use flip phones, it will take them awhile to accept this new system. Hopefully this will give young people the wealth redistribution that they so desperately need.

There are also currently a few companies working on cryptocurrencies that are backed by gold, which is an interesting concept. On one hand, a cryptocurrency backed by gold will likely have a price that is less subject to volatility than that of other cryptocurrencies. At the same time, what would stop governments in the future from trying to seize the gold? I am undecided if this is a good or bad idea, especially since there already are some bullion dealers that accept Bitcoin.

The future of cryptocurrency is largely dependent on the answer to three questions. Will governments and banks ban it? Will Ebay or Amazon honor it? Will our financial system fall apart? Every fiat currency that has ever existed has ultimately failed; cryptocurrency may be able to change that.

Personally, I believe that a worldwide payment system that is faster and more efficient than what we currently have will become more valuable than a company such as Apple. The current market cap of Apple is about $800 billion, I would not be surprised to see a single cryptocurrency obtain that type of evaluation. There are over $300 trillion between all nations, and if cryptocurrency can achieve even 3% of that, it would make the market cap $9 trillion, or about 18x what it currently is.

While the vast majority of this chapter focused on Bitcoin as it is the most well-known cryptocurrency, the future favors Ethereum the second largest cryptocurrency. Ethereum offers something called smart contracts and is being implemented by some of the largest companies in the world. These smart contracts are autonomous and can save companies millions of dollars in lawyer fees. Ethereum also has an underlying programming language that can be used by developers to create decentralized applications. Is this the technology that changes the future? Only time will tell.

Even if cryptocurrency somehow manages to fail, its technology will not be forgotten. Companies such as Walmart are attempting to develop a blockchain to help with food safety, while other companies such as Price Waterhouse Cooper is exploring its uses in the finance industry. In June 2017, IBM was tasked to build a blockchain-based international trading system for seven of the world's largest banks. Blockchain offers a more secure and efficient way to do go about many tasks, and it has the ability to save many companies millions or billions of dollars.

Moving forward, cryptocurrency and the technology behind it is just too important to be ignored. It has the ability to solve many problems, and can help level the playing field for younger people at a disadvantage. It has become increasingly concerning that in many cases a very small group of people or companies have so much power that they can control almost anything.

Isn't it time for people to take control of their money and not let banks and governments dictate what they can and cannot do?

CHAPTER 16

How a Poor Generation Can Invest For the Future

Just because something has never happened, doesn't mean that it won't, and just because something happened in the past, doesn't mean that it will happen again in the future. This said, history does tend to repeat itself. Fortunes will continue to be made and lost in America through investing. Everyone wants to be rich, but in our current system not everyone can win all the time.

I am not very fond of most of the work written by the academic community when it comes to finance or economics. This is largely because most academics are quite poor at making predictions. No one can predict the exact date in which a market will crash. For example, Robert J. Shiller, an American Nobel Laureate, economist has been noted as someone who has predicted a market crash many times in which it has happened only twice. He is not strikingly accurate with his predictions.

There is, however, one academic that I respect. I find his work to be valuable in predicting market crashes, and that is James Tobin of Yale University, Nobel laureate in economics. Tobin devised something called the Q ratio, where he hypothesized that the combined market value of all the companies on the stock market should be about equal to their replacement costs. The Q ratio is calculated as the market value of a company divided by the replacement value of the firm's assets.[175]

The Q ratio has reached over 1.0 on 5 separate occasions in history. The years that this threshold was crossed were 1906, 1929, 1937, 2000, and currently since about 2015, 4 of the 5 times that this ratio has crossed this mark, a massive stock market crash was soon to follow. While this may not be a prefect predictor of what will happen, this type of predictor does tell us that market is overvalued and that a price correction is most likely soon to follow. As of mid-March 2020, the Q ratio is the second highest in history at 2.04.[176]

One of the challenges with investing is the human behavior associated with investing. When an investment does well for years on end, people tend to get complacent. As things continue to rise, more people have the fear of missing out and this creates an investor frenzy. People start to think that the market is never going down and greed takes control of them. At some point investing becomes more like gambling than investing. This results in people taking greater and greater risks.

The stock market crash of 1929 is largely regarded as the worst economic collapse in U.S. history. While the cause of the crash is often debated among economists, most agree that one of the biggest contributing factors was people buying on margin and leveraging. These both refer to the same concept. Buying on margin is the purchase of an asset by using leverage and borrowing the balance from a bank or broker. Leveraging allows an individual to control larger trade sizes. Either way this refers to people buying things with money they don't have. Today, many investors are leveraging in the real estate market and the stock market.

A lot of young people get excited about real estate. After all, selling real estate and real estate investing has made more millionaires than any other form of investing in the world. The problem is that a lot of younger people get real-estate advice from YouTube stars like Grant

Cardone and Kevin Paffrath, aka Meet Kevin. These real estate "masters" talk about leveraging your money to buy real-estate. Grant Cardone talks about a deal where he took out a loan for $13.5 million with 0% down on a 25,000 sq. foot piece of property. He rationalizes that this is a good investment because he will be able to get a tenant that will pay $50 per square foot. This amounts to him earning $1,250,000 per year at the cost of $780,000 in debt.[177] Kevin talks about similar concepts in his videos on real estate. In one video he talks about controlling a $1.2 million property for $42k down. He suggests using an FHA loan where someone only needs to put 3.5% down and can control up to four units. He then suggests making the loan payments with the income from tenants.[178]

Grant and Kevin both think they are making great investments, but the investment style they present is very high risk. Both rely on real estate prices and rent prices to either increase or remain the same. In an instance where prices go down, the income they bring in from their tenants will not be able to cover their loans. In this circumstance, investors will essentially bleed money until they go bankrupt. The idea of leveraging in real estate is taking a major risk, because if there is a housing crisis like 2007, you will lose everything.

At the same time leveraging in the stock market is also a major problem. Currently, leverage and speculation in the market has reached historic highs. According to McAlvany Financial, since 2008, we have 40% more debt in the market relative to the world's total economy.[179] Advisorperspectives shows that there is nearly three times the negative credit balance held amongst investors than there was during the tech bubble.[180] There is clearly some high-risk behavior and a lot of hot money seeking returns in the market at present, but investor behavior isn't the only thing to be concerned about.

At the core of investing are stockbrokers and financial advisors.

These professions are often paid on commission only, or charge a fee based on the assets invested. If there is one thing you should have learned from this book by now, it is that incentives drive human behavior. While there are some really great honest and helpful professionals in the industry, there are also many stockbrokers and financial advisors who don't always act in their clients' best interests. Their goal is to get people to invest money, even when markets are overinflated and not many quality investment opportunities exist. At the same time, many advisors have deals with certain companies to promote their products, even if they suck. This often leads people in these professions to try and sell their clients insurances that aren't needed, stocks that are high risk and other services that are expensive and low value. Financial advisors also tend to lack a strong understanding of economics and have a hard time dealing with change. Many suggest investments that worked in the past, but as I stated earlier, that doesn't mean that these investments will also be successful in the future.

A lot of financial advisors push for elderly people in retirement to own a certain amount of "risk-free" assets such as treasury securities. U.S. treasury bills have been paraded for a long time as being an incredibly safe investment. Treasury securities are divided into three categories according to their lengths of maturities. These three classifications are T-bills, T-notes, and T-bonds. T-bills are government bonds that have a maturity of 4, 13, 26 and 52 weeks. T-Notes have maturity terms of 2, 3, 5, 7 and 10 years. T-bonds mature in thirty years. There are a few other differences between the three, but I intend only to focus on the basics. The face value of the bond, that is the value at which the issuer will redeem the bond at maturity (assuming it does not default) is called the par value. Most bonds are issued at par value. The interest you will receive on a bond is called a coupon rate. Now suppose you purchase a bond for

$1,000. You will receive a bond with par value of $1,000 and a coupon rate of 4%. This means that you will receive annual coupon payments of $40, and you will receive the $1,000 back when the bond matures.

Treasury securities are a debt instrument. In other words, you are essentially loaning out your money. Although treasuries can be bought by individual investors, most are bought by other sources. Pension plans, retirement funds, insurance companies, banks and broker-dealers, are the biggest purchasers of these treasury notes. In fact, U.S. government laws dictate that many of these organizations are required to have a certain amount of risk-free investments (T-bills/notes/bonds) in their holdings.

There are two issues with treasury securities. The first is that they have very low returns and significantly higher risk than they used to. It was discussed in a previous chapter just how problematic municipal bonds are, considering the debt at state level. This could lead to bankruptcy. One only needs to look at Detroit to see that bankruptcy can happen in a city. Of course, bankruptcy can easily happen at a state level which means that the government as a whole is in jeopardy too. Although the U.S. government has never defaulted on their bonds, this doesn't mean that default will never occur. The U.S. now stands a higher probability of defaulting than ever before.

The second problem with bonds has to do with interest rates and inflation rates. Why exactly would someone buy a bond with a 2% yield, when the inflation rate is 3%? In other words, why would you invest your money into something that you know will lose you money? For much of the last ten years, ten-year treasury rates have been lower than inflation. In fact, for the first time in financial history the FED has given us negative interest rates in recent years. When the FED raises interest rates you can expect higher mortgage rates, higher car loan rates, higher credit card rates, higher yields on treasury bonds, lower home sales, lower borrowing, lower consumer spending, and lower profits. When the FED lowers interest rates you can expect just the opposite. This, of course, could be a major problem if they raise rates too much and homeowners are unable to pay their mortgages. This was addressed in chapter 3.

Another major concern about bonds is that investors are extremely dependent on bond rating agencies. Moody's, S&P, and Fitch are responsible for more than 95% of global bond ratings.[181] As we saw in the 2007 financial crisis, these rating agencies gave completely inaccurate ratings to mortgage-backed securities, and many people lost money. This was especially highlighted in The Big Short, which is both a movie and a book. This has led investors to be more concerned about a conflict of interest between the rating agencies and the bond issuers, since the issuers pay the agencies for the service of providing ratings.

Much of this book is about how young people are at a disadvantage, and how our current systems make problems worse. It also explains that the massive debt bubble in the economy and financial markets is unsustainable. Unfortunately, there is no way to determine when this bubble will burst, but what can people do in the meantime? How can young people close the wealth gap, increase their quality of life and level the playing field in today's society?

It starts with making sacrifices and intelligent decisions in investing. But what exactly are the sacrifices that someone should make, and what investments are a good idea? The truth is that younger generations will need to engage in very different investments than previous generations to balance the wealth. This chapter formulates opinions and predications based on the other chapters in this book. I am not an investment professional, but I can see the challenges that the economy is facing.

Much of this book talks about cause and effect relationships.

While some laws or changes to the economy are felt immediately, others can take many years to experience the full impact. For example, nearing the release date of this book, COVID-19 is making headlines across the world and creating panic, death and chaos. It is unclear what the final result of it will be, but there have been immediate effects and most likely more effects to come in the future. An earlier chapter focused on Social Security and welfare, which are prime examples of long term effects. When these programs were introduced in the 1930s they worked fine, but due to their dependencies they started to experience problems in the 1970s when people started to have significantly fewer children. With fewer children, we experienced a smaller working class and a need to support too many people in retirement. Newton's third law is: For every action, there is an equal and opposite reaction. This is the same with economics. When investing in today's economy it is important to formulate cause and effect relationships and also look at incentives.

America is a debt-based economy that has an obsession with paper. This includes paper money, paper stock shares, and promises written on paper. Investing in a big company through the stock market allows you very little control over the company and what it actually produces. Stocks and bonds have a high level of liquidity, which means that you can turn them into cash easily, but they also prone to flash crashes where they lose a significant amount of value in a short amount of time. Is the opportunity for a low return worth the risk of losing half of your paper assets?

It is my viewpoint that most investments in the overinflated and overleveraged market are highly risky at this point in time. Over the next few years it is probable that America will be moving away from a debt-based economy to an asset-based economy. In this circumstance ownership of a resource or productive method will be valued significantly more than it is now. Smart investments are in tangible resources like commodities. This includes raw material or agricultural products that people will always need. Arable farmland, silver, gold, oil, and firearms are great examples of this.

One of the greatest obsessions Americans have is owning real estate. Unfortunately, it is expensive and people are often owned by their property and not the other way around. The risk is that the market is greatly overinflated and most types of real estate produce nothing. Condos and apartments are a great example of expensive property that doesn't create anything. These are poor investments at the current time. Value is found in land that has utility, such as arable farmland. Farmland is a good investment because you can plant and grow food, which gives you actual tangible resources. People will always need food. Food will always have value. The emergence of COVID-19 should serve as a wakeup call as it is leaving store shelves empty and shows just how fragile our food supply chain is. Taking out excessive debt to buy an apartment is high risk because markets are too high and it is quite possible that you will have more debt in a property than what it is worth.

Another thing that will always have value is silver and gold. In Chapter 13, it was mentioned that these act as a fullproof storage of wealth. These precious metals have outlived every fiat currency in existence and have been valued for over 2,000 years. In addition, silver has heavy industrial demand in a huge array of electronic devices, and gold can be used in jewelry, aerospace and the medical world. Since the year 2000, there have been thirteen years of silver shortages, yet the price continues to stay low. This is mainly due to price manipulation caused by central banking authorities as well as technology companies that do not want to see the prices rise, as it will make manufacturing more expensive. A great example of this manipulation can be seen at the beginning of COVID-19 where silver prices fell to less than $12 dollars an ounce. This low price would suggest a low demand, but all bullion dealers were completely sold out and it was almost impossible to get your hands on any silver at all. There was such a shortage that many dealers started to impose premiums on bars of up to $4 an ounce. Does it make sense for paper trading to influence physical prices when it is so difficult to obtain the physical item? Artificially low prices for silver create an environment in which fewer mining companies find it profitable to continue to mine. Increased demand due to industrial needs, less supply, and low prices show that the price has nowhere to go but up in the future. At the current price of approximately 15$ an ounce, silver is highly undervalued.

When it comes to owning silver and gold, I would suggest owning tangible bullion (bars) and putting them in a secure home safe. This is smarter than buying paper shares through the stock market because the prices of the paper are subject to manipulation and do not necessarily reflect an asset's actual price. It is difficult to believe that 75 ounces of silver have the same value as one ounce of gold when approximately ten ounces of silver come out of the ground for every one ounce of gold. There is clear market manipulation at play here. At the same time, it is possible that countries around the world move back to a gold standard form of currency in which paper money is once again backed by gold. This would only increase prices further. However, people should also be cautious of storing their silver or gold in a bank because the bank could go out of business or the government could seize all silver and gold like they did in the early 1900s.

Investing in oil is another possibility. Oil is one industry that will have a major impact on the economy within the next few years. After prices of crude oil hit $156.48 per barrel in June 2008, companies were making record profits and loving every second of it. But, after a wellhead on a BP deep-sea drilling platform blew up and caused the Deepwater Horizon oil spill in 2010, many more regulations combined with a decreased price hurt a lot of the smaller oil providers. In April 2020, Crude prices hit $0.01. Increasing costs, decreasing profits, decreased demand and more regulations have led many of the smaller offshore oil platform companies to financial strain. Ocean Rig UDW Inc. an operator of semisubmersible oil rigs and UDW drillships is one of many companies that may soon face possible bankruptcy. With all the strain on the industry, and less enthusiasm about it, oil discoveries are now at a 70-year low. In the next few years when the demand for oil goes back up, we will experience sky high oil prices and new companies will join the market because of profits and increased demand.

Guns and ammunition present another unique investment opportunity. They can be used for personal enjoyment, hunting, self-defense or competition. Some people also collect them and view them as a storage of wealth or investment similar to that of precious metals. Many guns also get handed through generations as they tend to last a long time and retain their value if well maintained. Some people also advocate stockpiling bullets, because in the event of economic collapse they believe bullets could be used as a currency. In an ammunition shortage, bullets could become very valuable. Most people fail to realize just how close we were to a complete financial collapse in 2007–2008. We were literally only a few weeks from being forced back into a farming lifestyle. With the rise of technology and the decades of easy living it has provided, many people have forgotten old skills such as hunting and living off the land. Perhaps these may again become valuable skills someday.

The last investment I wanted to talk about in this chapter is cryptocurrency. Cryptocurrency such as Bitcoin and Ethereum is the only intangible investment I would recommend. While it may experience high levels of volatility, crypto provides some substantial advantages in comparison to the dollar. It cannot be subject to fraudulent transactions like a credit card, it cannot be printed infinitely, and it cannot be directly controlled by a bank or government entity.

While there is a degree of speculation in cryptocurrency, the risk of it becoming worthless is almost nonexistent because this would require every user in the world to agree it is worthless. The potential reward of owning Bitcoin or Ethereum could result in very high rewards. While Bitcoin may not be the crypto of the future that unites all countries in the world under one banner, at this point it is unlikely to simply fade away. I would recommend investing in multiple cryptocurrencies to minimize risk. At the end of the day, digital money is the future, and the crypto that solves the most problems will most likely become the first currency used across all countries and cultures. At this point in time the cryptocurrencies Bitcoin, Ethereum, EOS and IOTA all seem like possible candidates to lead the world forward.

This chapter highlights just a few investments and the reasoning for why they may be good decisions in the future, but it ultimately aims to get people to think about investing in a different way. For many years if you invested any money into almost any stock in the stock market you made money, but that time is coming to an end. In today's world the people who will benefit the most will be those that think differently about investing and do research. Too many people rush into an investment without having a real reason why they want to invest in it. If you don't have an understanding of what you're buying, you probably shouldn't buy it. In the end, much of the younger generation in America needs to start thinking about investing and making decisions to try and obtain a better future. Working a regular 9 to 5 job just isn't enough anymore.

CHAPTER 17

Conclusion

One of the best interviews I've ever heard was with Seth Godin, author of The Icarus Deception. Many children grow up hearing the story of Icarus. The version they hear is "Don't fly too close to the sun or your wax will melt and you'll die," but this isn't the original myth according to Godin. The original myth was: "Don't fly too close to the sun or your wax will melt and you'll die, but more important, don't fly too low. If you fly too low, the waves will weigh you down and you will perish." When asked further about this, Seth replied:

> "I think we're guilty of flying too low. I think we've built this unbelievable, connected economy, this infrastructure, and yet we're all sitting around playing silly games, watching cat videos and day trading when we could be doing something really important and risky, and things that matter. That's what I want to see happen."[182]

I am in agreement with Godin. There are a lot of people from my generation on platforms like YouTube, but almost none stand for anything of actual importance. What we need are young people who are willing to go against the grain. We need people who want to make lives better and who want to invest time into something greater than themselves. It is through this constant pursuit of innovation and challenging the status quo that America has got to where it is today.

What worries me the most is that newer generations may have lost this ability. Today's youth experience increased financial challenges and have become increasingly docile. Rather than fight against political gridlock, low wages, poverty, and a system that forces people to live paycheck to paycheck, young people have done nothing. The reality is that we can do so much better than this mediocre lifestyle that is gradually leading us closer to a society where the common worker represents a slave.

America's new norm is millennials living with their parents into their 30s, college graduates working for poverty wages, and a wealth distribution where only a handful of people can live a high quality life. The challenge is that current financial circumstances have forced millennials to give up many real world experiences. For instance, travel experiences have now been replaced with virtual experiences that young people gain from playing video games. Meanwhile, today's young people are often characterized by the older generation as lazy, naïve losers who want to change the world.

The truth is that this is a generation of people hungry for achievement with limited paths to get there.

Perhaps the hardest thing for millennials to deal with was seeing their expectations fall far short of reality. They were told that if they obeyed the rules, got good grades and worked hard, they would be rewarded fairly and evenly. The problem is that many millennials have gone deep into debt and have ultimately ended up working at a dead end job, or for their parents.

The one thing that made America the best country in the world for so long was the opportunity to become successful regardless of where you came from. The idea was that it is in every person's power to achieve greatness with hard work and dedication. The disturbing reality is that the majority of young people are more dependent on the success of their parents and grandparents than they are on their own ability to achieve success. In the age where so many young people are readily entertained by their electronic devices, one has to question whether newer generations will ever stand up and demand a better quality life. If millennials are unable to save up their money in the short term, how are they to reach the long term where they own houses, are successful and have children?

To move forward, we need to remove the barriers and lies in society. There needs to be more than just the false promise that someday young people will own something. In today's society there is increasing pressure on people to move out of the cities they grew up in because of the excessively high cost of living. It is unfortunate that younger people suffer so that the older generation can maintain their standard of living. Baby boomers were given by their parents the most prosperous nation in history and gradually through their overconsumption of resources and voting habits created a lifestyle that would come at the expense of later generations.

Perhaps one could argue that the biggest problem that America has is the fear of change, the fear of trying something new, and the fear of failing. I want my generation to shake things up and take risks to break the cycle that we are currently headed into. I want to see people break new ground and try new things, even if they fail. In ten or twenty years I want millennials to be proud of the path they have made, not reliant on an inheritance.

An old proverb said "Give a man a fish and you feed him for a day; teach a man to fish and you feed him for a lifetime." My goal with this book was to raise the conversation about a lot of the problems we have in today's society, and also give people the understanding of how we can deal with those problems. I can't make people act, but I can help to get people to think for themselves.

I want this book to open people's eyes to the issues around them, bridge the generation gap, and inspire other young people to make a difference and fight for a better quality of life. Throughout history, young people have done amazing things.

In ancient Greece, a teenage prince from Macedonia became one of the most powerful influencers in history. When King Philip died at the hand of his own bodyguard, it was his son, Alexander, who took control of the throne in 336 B.C. During a time when Greece was more divided than ever, Alexander would unite the Greeks, free the Greek colonies from the Persians, and ultimately overthrow the Persian Empire. He became known as Alexander the Great.

In the early 1400s a 16-year-old girl named Joan of Arc made an unlikely journey to speak with the Dauphin of France. Her visit sparked the French leader to renew the conflict with the English. This decision would eventually lead to the independence of France.

In the early 1920s a 14-year-old farm boy gifted in chemistry and physics started to work on an invention. Seven years later, in 1927, Philo Farnsworth developed and patented the world's first fully electronic television.

In February of 2004 a group of Harvard students made a website designed to connect select college campuses together. This would eventually become something much greater and Facebook was born. Little did people know that social media would become one of the strongest forces in the world, revolutionizing the way we communicate and collect information.

All of these people changed the world. Now more than ever, America needs young voices to challenge bad processes and to fight for a progressive future.

Section III: Five Keys to Success

The third section of this book explored the challenges associated with wealth distribution and investing. How might someone address these problems? Here are five ideas that people can use to improve their lives and address the challenges discussed in chapters 11 through 17.

1) **Avoid Storing Too Much in a Bank:** Banks can be very dangerous places because fractional reserve lending does not work. The banking system nearly failed during the great depression and again in 2008. You may wake up one morning unable to access your money or your safety deposit box. The FDIC does not have enough money to insure every bank account in America. You should keep only a small amount in these institutions and use the rest for tangible investing. Stay away from having too much cash.

2) **Buy a Safe:** Buying a home safe and hiding it or disguising it can protect you and put you in a place where you are far more prepared than others. Put several thousand dollars of cash in the safe as an emergency fund and use it to store your valuables.

3) **Buy Precious Metals:** Everyone should own at least a small amount of gold and silver bullion. No matter the time in history, precious metals have always held purchasing power. They are the safest storage of wealth in existence and a great insurance policy against things going wrong. Check out reputable online dealers like JM Bullion or APMEX and store your precious metals in a secure home safe.

4) **Investigate Digital Currency:** Cryptocurrency represents an investment opportunity with high volatility where there is high risk and high reward. I cannot tell you which cryptocurrency will rule the world, but I can tell you that we are going digital;

it's only a matter of time. If you have a few dollars lying around consider investing in a crypto like Bitcoin or Ethereum. You may very well be able to buy a house for a single coin in the future.

5) **Obtain Real Estate:** When the market goes down and becomes affordable real estate can be a great investment. The two certainties about real estate are that rent never seems to go down and land will always have value. Buy low and sell high. Use your land to create something and don't waste it. Having a rental property is in my opinion better than having a bunch of money in the stock market.

References

CHAPTER 1

[1]   Tavernise, S. (2016, April 22). U.S. Suicide Rate Surges to a 30-Year High. New York Times.
•Retrieved from https://www.nytimes.com/2016/04/22/health/us-suicide-rate-surges-to-a-30-year-high.html

[2]   Pratt, Ph.D, L. A., Brody, M.P.H, D. J., & Gu. M.D., Ph.D, Q. (2011). NCHS Data Brief (76).
•Retrieved from National Center for Health Statistics website:
https://www.cdc.gov/nchs/products/databriefs/db76.htm

[3]   Gopal, P. (2016, July 28). Homeownership rate in the U.S. drops to lowest since 1965.
•Retrieved from https://www.bloomberg.com/news/articles/2016-07-28/homeownership-rate-in-the-u-s-tumbles-to-the-lowest-since-1965

CHAPTER 2

[4]   Statista. (2018). U.S. retail price of sliced bacon, 2017 | statistic.
•Retrieved from https://www.statista.com/statistics/236811/retail-price-of-sliced-bacon-in-the-united-states/

[5]   Northrup, L. (2014, April 23). Sun Chips Bags Shrink From 10 Ounces To 7 Ounces, Price Stays The Same.
•Retrieved from https://consumerist.com/2014/04/23/sun-chips-bags-shrink-from-10-5-ounces-to-7-ounces-price-stays-the-same/

[6]   Traffic / Toll Data. (n.d.).
•Retrieved from http://goldengatebridge.org/research/GGBTraffToll.php

[7]   Hedgpeth, D., & Lazo, L. (2017, December 5). I-66 toll hits $40 on Day 2. Virginia transportation chief: 'No one has to pay a toll.' The Washington Post.
•Retrieved from https://www.washingtonpost.com/news/dr-gridlock/wp/2017/12/05/i-66-toll-in-virginia-reaches-new-high-of-36-50-on-day-2/?utm_term=.84e3cce6098f

[8]   United States Department of Transportation. (n.d.). Table 11-5 Toll Roads, Bridges and Tunnels.
•Retrieved from bureau of transportation statistics website:
https://www.bts.gov/bts/archive/publications/north_american_transportation_in_figures/table_11_5

[9]   United States Department of Transportation. (2016). Total Toll Road, Toll Bridge, and Toll Tunnel Length in Operation as of January 1, 2015.
•Retrieved from federal highway administration website:
https://www.fhwa.dot.gov/policyinformation/tollpage/factsheet.cfm

[10]   Desta, Y. (2015, March 22). 1904 to today: See how New York City subway fare has climbed over 111 years.
•Retrieved from http://mashable.com/2015/03/22/new-york-city-subway-fare/#J2cuGqxHYPqc

[11]   Lindblom, M. (2010, December 29). Coming soon: parking rates that go up at busiest times.
•Retrieved from http://www.seattletimes.com/seattle-news/coming-soon-parking-rates-that-go-up-at-busiest-times/

[12]   Study: Parking Costs Angelenos $3.7 Billion A Year. (2017, July 13).

•Retrieved from http://losangeles.cbslocal.com/2017/07/13/parking-costs-angelenos-3-7-billion-a-year/

[13]   The American Automobile Association. (1995). Your driving costs.
•Retrieved from https://exchange.aaa.com/wp-content/uploads/2015/08/1995-YDC-Final.pdf

[14]   The American Automobile Association. (2015). Your driving costs.
•Retrieved from https://exchange.aaa.com/wp-content/uploads/2015/04/Your-Driving-Costs-2015.pdf

[15]   CollegeBoard. (2018). Tuition and fees and room and board over time—trends in higher education.
•Retrieved from https://trends.collegeboard.org/college-pricing/figures-tables/tuition-fees-room-and-board-over-time

[16]   Kellermann, A., & Auerbach, D. (2017, August 2). A Decade Of Health Care Cost Growth Has Wiped Out Real Income Gains For An Average US Family | Health Affairs.
•Retrieved from https://www.healthaffairs.org/doi/abs/10.1377/hlthaff.2011.0585

[17]   Journal of Patient Safety. (2013, March). March 2013—Volume 9—Issue 1 : Journal of Patient Safety.
•Retrieved from https://journals.lww.com/journalpatientsafety/toc/2013/03000

[18]   Jena, M.D., Ph.D., A., Seabury, Ph.D., S., Lakdawalla, Ph.D., D., & Chandra, Ph.D., A. (2011, August 17). Malpractice risk according to physician specialty | NEJM.
•Retrieved from https://www.nejm.org/doi/full/10.1056/NEJMsa1012370

[19]   Becker Law Firm. (2016, June 16). 10 biggest medical malpractice payouts.
•Retrieved from https://www.ohio-birthinjurylawyers.com/medical-malpractice/2016/06/10-biggest-medical-malpractice-payouts/

[20]   Massachusetts Institute of Technology. (2015, March 18). Study: Prices of cancer drugs have soared since 1995.
•Retrieved from http://news.mit.edu/2015/cancer-drug-prices-rise-10-percent-annually-0318

[21]   Hays, J. (Director). (2012). Doctored: the film the AMA does not want you to see [Motion picture]. CA: Jeff Hays Films.

[22]   International Federation of Health Plans. (2015). 2015 comparative price report variation in medical and hospital prices by country.
•Retrieved from https://docplayer.net/48892596-2015-comparative-price-report-variation-in-medical-and-hospital-prices-by-country.html

[23]   Kaiser Health News. (2017, April 17). In Trump's first quarter, pharma companies doubled their lobbying spending.
•Retrieved from https://www.healthcarefinancenews.com/news/trumps-first-quarter-pharma-companies-doubled-their-lobbying-spending

[24]   U.S. Census Bureau, Housing and Household Economic Statistics Division. (2011). Historical census of housing tables—gross rents.
•Retrieved from U.S. Census Bureau website:
https://www.census.gov/hhes/www/housing/census/historic/grossrents.html

[25]   Rent Cafe. (2020). Average Rent in San Francisco & Rent Prices by Neighborhood—RENTCafé.
•Retrieved from https://www.rentcafe.com/average-rent-market-trends/us/ca/san-francisco/

[26]   Giever, E., Stoughton, K. M., & Loper, S. (n.d.). Analysis of Water Rate Escalations across the United States.
•Retrieved from department of energy website:
https://energy.gov/sites/prod/files/2013/10/f3/pnnl_80989.pdf

[27] Disneyland Annual Passport Price Over Time | Ultimate Guide. (2019).
      •Retrieved from http://www.mousemonthly.com/ultimate-disney-guides/disneyland-resort-annual-passes/ap-price-history/

[28] Cordcutting. (2016, November 1). Cable prices have risen at more than double the rate of inflation for 20 years.
      •Retrieved from https://boingboing.net/2016/11/01/cable-prices-have-risen-at-mor.html

[29] Average NFL ticket price 2006–2016 | Statistic. (n.d.).
      •Retrieved from https://www.statista.com/statistics/193425/average-ticket-price-in-the-nfl-since-2006/

CHAPTER 3

[30] Federal Reserve Bank of New York. (2018). Household Debt And Credit.
      •Retrieved from https://www.newyorkfed.org/medialibrary/interactives/householdcredit/data/pdf/HHDC_2018Q1.pdf

[31] U.S. Census Bureau. (2011). Historical census of housing tables—Homeownership.
      •Retrieved from https://www.census.gov/hhes/www/housing/census/historic/owner.html

[32] US Census Bureau. (2012). Historical census of housing tables home values.
      •Retrieved from https://www.census.gov/hhes/www/housing/census/historic/values.html

[33] Social Security Administration. (2017). Average wages, median wages, and wage dispersion.
      •Retrieved from https://www.ssa.gov/oact/cola/central.html

[34] Federal Reserve Bank Of St. Louis. (2017, December 14). 30-Year Fixed Rate Mortgage Average in the United States | FRED | St. Louis Fed.
      •Retrieved from https://fred.stlouisfed.org/graph/?g=NUh

[35] Federal Reserve Bank Of St. Louis. (2017, November 27). Median Sales Price for New Houses Sold in the United States.
      •Retrieved from https://fred.stlouisfed.org/series/MSPNHSUS

[36] Board Of Governors Of The Federal Reserve System. (2017). Mortgage Debt Outstanding (Table 1.54).
      •Retrieved from https://www.federalreserve.gov/data/mortoutstand/current.htm

[37] Yun, L. (2017). Realtors Confidence Index Survey.
      •Retrieved from National Association Of Realtors website: https://www.nar.realtor/sites/default/files/reports/2017/2017-02-realtors-confidence-index-03-22-2017.pdf

[38] The Institute for Higher Education Policy, Sallie Mae Education Institute, & The Education Resources Institute. (1997). Student Loan Debt: Problems & Prospects.
      •Retrieved from http://www.ihep.org/sites/default/files/uploads/docs/pubs/studentloandebt.pdf

[39] Digangi, C. (2016, May 6). The class of 2016 will graduate with an average of $37,172 in debt.
      •Retrieved from https://www.foxbusiness.com/features/the-class-of-2016-will-graduate-with-an-average-of-37172-in-debt

[40] Weinstein, A. (2017, June 25). How pricey for-profit colleges target vets' GI Bill money.
      •Retrieved from http://www.motherjones.com/politics/2011/09/gi-bill-for-profit-colleges

[41] Federal Reserve Bank Of St. Louis. (2017, December 7). Motor Vehicle Loans Owned and Securitized, Outstanding.
      •Retrieved from https://alfred.stlouisfed.org/series?seid=MVLOAS&utm_source=series_page&utm_medium=related_content&utm_term=related_resources&utm_campaign=alfred

[42]   Zabritski, M. (2015). State of the Automotive Finance Market Second Quarter 2015.
•Retrieved from Experian Information Solutions website:
https://www.experian.com/assets/automotive/white-papers/experian-auto-2015-q2.pdf?WT.srch=Auto_Q12015FinanceTrends_PDF

[43]   Sestric, L. (2018, January 25). Here's how much a $35,263 car today would cost the year you were born.
•Retrieved from https://www.gobankingrates.com/saving-money/car/heres-much-car-today-would-cost-year-were-born/#5

[44]   Edmunds.Com. (2016). H1 2016 LEASE MARKET.
•Retrieved from https://static.ed.edmunds-media.com/unversioned/img/industry-center/analysis/h1-2016-lease-report.pdf

CHAPTER 4

[45]   Economic Policy Institute. (2018, August). The productivity pay gap.
•Retrieved from https://www.epi.org/productivity-pay-gap/

[46]   Berman, J. (2018, April 21). The net worth of college graduates with student debt is truly depressing.
•Retrieved from https://www.marketwatch.com/story/the-net-worth-of-college-graduates-with-student-debt-is-truly-depressing-2018-04-19

[47]   Shapiro, B. (2015, December 11). Ben Shapiro at Otay Ranch High School [Video file].
•Retrieved from https://www.youtube.com/watch?v=_5FeZE4O_XU&feature=youtu.be&t=1638

[48]   Career Builder. (2017, August 24). Living paycheck to paycheck is a way of life for majority of U.S. workers, according to new CareerBuilder survey.
•Retrieved from http://press.careerbuilder.com/2017-08-24-Living-Paycheck-to-Paycheck-is-a-Way-of-Life-for-Majority-of-U-S-Workers-According-to-New-CareerBuilder-Survey

[49]   Dixon, A. (2018, June 25). Survey: the average side hustler earns over $8K annually | Bankrate.com.
•Retrieved from https://www.bankrate.com/personal-finance/smart-money/side-hustles-survey-june-2018/

[50]   Hours, S. (2014, August 29). The "40-hour" workweek is actually longer.
•Retrieved from https://news.gallup.com/poll/175286/hour-workweek-actually-longer-seven-hours.aspx

[51]   Mishel, L. (2013, January 30). Vast majority of wage earners are working harder, and for not much more: trends in U.S. work hours and wages over 1979–2007.
•Retrieved from https://www.epi.org/publication/ib348-trends-us-work-hours-wages-1979-2007/

[52]   Green, D. (2017, October 19). Timberland reveals a depressing truth about millennials' future in a new ad.
•Retrieved from https://www.businessinsider.com/timberland-ad-millennials-2017-10

[53]   Statistic Brain. (2017, September 22). Retirement Statistics.
•Retrieved from http://www.statisticbrain.com/retirement-statistics/

[54]   National Center for Health Statistics. (2018). NCHS data visualization gallery – natality trends in the United States.
•Retrieved from https://www.cdc.gov/nchs/data-visualization/natality-trends/

[55]   Bretz, L. (2018, April 2). As rents rise, more renters turn to doubling Up—Zillow Research.
•Retrieved from https://www.zillow.com/research/rising-rents-more-roommates-17618/

[56] Cohn, D., & Passel, J. (2018, April 5). Record 64 million Americans live in multigenerational households.
      •Retrieved from http://www.pewresearch.org/fact-tank/2018/04/05/a-record-64-million-americans-live-in-multigenerational-households/

CHAPTER 5

[57] Kiersz, A. (2018, November 20). Here's what the typical American worker earns at every age.
      •Retrieved from https://www.businessinsider.com/typical-salary-americans-at-every-age-2018-6

[58] OneWisconsin Institute. (2014, June 24). Twenty to life: Higher ed turning into multi- decade debt sentence.
      •Retrieved from https://onewisconsinnow.org/press/twenty-to-life-higher-education-turning-into-multi-decade-debt-sentence/

[59] PayScale.com. (2020). 2019–20 College Salary Report.
      •Retrieved from https://www.payscale.com/college-salary-report/majors-that-pay-you-back

[60] Accenture. (2015). Accenture 2015 college graduate employment survey [table].
      •Retrieved from http://i.huffpost.com/gen/2940790/original.jpg

[61] Complete College America. (n.d.). The college completion crisis.
      •Retrieved from https://completecollege.org/

[62] Torpey, E. (2018, April 10). Measuring the value of education : Career outlook.
      •Retrieved from U.S. Bureau of Labor Statistics website:
      https://www.bls.gov/careeroutlook/2018/data-on-display/education-pays.htm

[63] National Center for Education Statistics. (2019). The condition of education—International comparisons—Enrollment and attainment—International educational attainment.
      •Retrieved from https://nces.ed.gov/programs/coe/indicator_cac.asp

[64] University entrance qualification. (n.d.).
      •Retrieved from https://www.study-in-germany.de/en/plan-your-studies/requirements/university-entrance-qualification_27788.php

[65] Lundberg, C. (2006, February 6). France's higher-ed system is more egalitarian and more elitist than ours.
      •Retrieved from https://slate.com/business/2014/02/higher-education-in-france-lots-of-testing-lots-of-planning-not-lots-of-money.html

[66] National Center for Education Statistics. (2019). The condition of education—International comparisons—Finances—Education expenditures by country.
      •Retrieved from https://nces.ed.gov/programs/coe/indicator_cmd.asp

[67] The World Bank. (n.d.). Military expenditure (% of GDP).
      •Retrieved
      https://data.worldbank.org/indicator/MS.MIL.XPND.GD.ZS?most_recent_value_desc=true

CHAPTER 6

[68] National Low Income Housing Coalition. (2018). Out of reach 2018.
      •Retrieved from https://nlihc.org/sites/default/files/oor/OOR_2018.pdf

[69] U.S. Bureau of Labor Statistics. (2018, March 22). Characteristics of minimum wage workers, 2017 (1072).
      •Retrieved from https://www.bls.gov/opub/reports/minimum-wage/2017/home.htm

[70] Casselman, B. (2015, October 8). It's getting harder to move beyond a minimum-wage job.
      •Retrieved from https://fivethirtyeight.com/features/its-getting-harder-to-move-beyond-a-minimum-wage-job/

[71]   United States Department Of Labor. (n.d.). History of Federal Minimum Wage Rates Under the Fair Labor Standards Act, 1938–2009.
        •Retrieved from https://www.dol.gov/whd/minwage/chart.htm

[72]   National Bureau of Economic Research. (2017, June). Minimum wage increases, wages, and low-wage employment: evidence from Seattle.
        •Retrieved from https://evans.uw.edu/sites/default/files/NBER%20Working%20Paper.pdf

[73]   Li, S. (2017, February 28). Wendy's adds automation to the fast-food menu. Los Angeles Times.
        •Retrieved from http://www.latimes.com/business/la-fi-wendys-kiosk-20170227-story.html

[74]   Krogstad, J. M., Passel, J. S., & Cohn, D. (2019, June 12). 5 facts about illegal immigration in the U.S.
        •Retrieved from https://www.pewresearch.org/fact-tank/2017/04/27/5-facts-about-illegal-immigration-in-the-u-s/

[75]   Barboza, D. (2001, December 20). Tyson Foods Indicted in Plan To Smuggle Illegal Workers. New York Times.
        •Retrieved from http://www.nytimes.com/2001/12/20/us/tyson-foods-indicted-in-plan-to-smuggle-illegal-workers.html

[76]   Breitbart. (2016, July 25). Vegan Food Company Fined $1.5 Million for Hiring Illegal Aliens.
        •Retrieved from http://www.breitbart.com/texas/2016/07/25/vegan-food-company-fined-1-5-million-hiring-illegal-aliens/

[77]   Borjas, G. J. (2016, September/October). Yes, Immigration Hurts American Workers. Politico, 3(5), 2.
        •Retrieved from https://www.politico.com/magazine/story/2016/09/trump-clinton-immigration-economy-unemployment-jobs-214216

[78]   The Department of Licensing and Regulatory Affairs. (n.d.). LARA—New Minimum Wage for Michigan Employees.
        •Retrieved from http://www.michigan.gov/lara/0,4601,7-154-59886-370158--,00.html

[79]   United States Department Of Labor. (2016, November 7). Local Area Unemployment Statistics.
        •Retrieved from Bureau Of Labor Statistics website: https://www.bls.gov/lau/ptable14full2017.pdf

[80]   Oregon.gov. (n.d.). Oregon Minimum Wage Rate Summary.
        •Retrieved from http://www.oregon.gov/boli/whd/omw/pages/minimum-wage-rate-summary.aspx

[81]   McGowan, K. (2017, March 20). Nevada's Two-Tier Minimum Wage Law Survives Challenge. Bloomberg News.
        •Retrieved from https://www.bna.com/nevadas-twotier-minimum-n57982085461/

[82]   GFP. (2017). Defense Spending by Country.
        •Retrieved from https://www.globalfirepower.com/defense-spending-budget.asp

[83]   Segalman, R. (1986). Welfare and dependency in Switzerland.
        •Retrieved from
        https://www.nationalaffairs.com/storage/app/uploads/public/58e/1a4/d6b/58e1a4d6ba4dc470307219.pdf

[84]   World Population Review. (2018). US states—ranked by population 2018.
        •Retrieved from http://worldpopulationreview.com/states/

[85]   Stanford University. (2016, September 27). Stanford GSB Introduces MBA Fellowship for Midwesterners.
        •Retrieved from https://www.gsb.stanford.edu/newsroom/school-news/stanford-gsb-introduces-mba-fellowship-midwesterners

CHAPTER 7

[86] Federal Reserve Bank Of St. Louis. (2017, November 27). Median Sales Price for New Houses Sold in the United States.
•Retrieved from https://fred.stlouisfed.org/series/MSPNHSUS

[87] Social Security Administration. (2017). Average wages, median wages, and wage dispersion.
•Retrieved from https://www.ssa.gov/oact/cola/central.html

[88] Desilver, D. (2016, June 20). More older Americans are working than in recent years.
•Retrieved from http://www.pewresearch.org/fact-tank/2016/06/20/more-older-americans-are-working-and-working-more-than-they-used-to/

[89] American Staffing Association. (n.d.). Staffing Industry Statistics.
•Retrieved from https://americanstaffing.net/staffing-research-data/fact-sheets-analysis-staffing-industry-trends/staffing-industry-statistics/

[90] Bureau of Labor Statistics Data. (2020).
•Retrieved from https://data.bls.gov/timeseries/LNS12000000

[91] U.S. Census Bureau. (2017). Nativity and citizenship status in the United States (B05001).
•Retrieved from 2016 American Community Survey 1-Year Estimates website: https://data.census.gov/cedsci/table?q=U.S.%20Census%20Bureau.%20%282017%29.%20Nativity%20and%20citizenship%20status%20in%20the%20United%20States%20%28B05001%29.&g=0100000US_0500000US17011&hidePreview=false&tid=ACSDT5Y2017.B05001&t=Citizenship&y=2017&vintage=2017&layer=VT_2017_050_00_PY_D1&cid=B05001_001E

[92] May, C. (2015, October 27). Report: 75 Percent of U.S. Population Growth Since 2000 Due to Immigration. Breitbart.
•Retrieved from http://www.breitbart.com/big-government/2015/10/27/report-75-percent-u-s-population-growth-since-2000-due-immigration/

[93] United States Department Of Labor. (2017). Foreign-born Workers: Labor Force Characteristics Summary (USDL-17-0618).
•Retrieved from Bureau Of Labor Statistics website: https://www.bls.gov/news.release/forbrn.nr0.htm

[94] Najar, N. (2011, October 13). Squeezed out in India, students turn to United States.
•Retrieved from https://www.nytimes.com/2011/10/14/world/asia/squeezed-out-in-india-students-turn-to-united-states.html

[95] Ruiz, N., & Krogstad, J. M. (2018, March 29). Where most H-1B visa workers are located in the U.S.
•Retrieved from http://www.pewresearch.org/fact-tank/2018/03/29/h-1b-visa-approvals-by-us-metro-area/

[96] Statistic Brain. (2017, March 6). Job Overseas Outsourcing Statistics.
•Retrieved from https://www.statisticbrain.com/outsourcing-statistics-by-country/

[97] Fontinelle, A. (2003, November 25). Trickle-Down Theory. In Investopedia.
•Retrieved from http://www.investopedia.com/terms/t/trickledowntheory.asp

CHAPTER 8

[98] Amadeo, K. (2018, July 4). What Obama Budgeted in 2016 and What Congress Spent.
•Retrieved from https://www.thebalance.com/fy-2016-federal-budget-3882293

[99] Amadeo, K. (2020, April 19). Who really pays Uncle Sam's bills?
•Retrieved from https://www.thebalance.com/current-u-s-federal-government-tax-revenue-3305762

[100] Fontinelle, A. (2017, November 6). The History Of Taxes In The U.S.
•Retrieved from https://www.investopedia.com/articles/tax/10/history-taxes.asp

[101]   Brin, D. (2017, April 4). Taking the sting out of medical school debt.
       •Retrieved from https://news.aamc.org/medical-education/article/taking-sting-out-of-medical-school-debt/

[102]   Internal Revenue Service. (2018, October 16). 2018 federal tax rates, personal exemptions, & standard deductions.
       •Retrieved from https://www.irs.com/articles/2018-federal-tax-rates-personal-exemptions-and-standard-deductions

[103]   Desilver, D. (2017, October 6). A closer look at who does (and doesn't) pay U.S. income tax.
       •Retrieved from http://www.pewresearch.org/fact-tank/2017/10/06/a-closer-look-at-who-does-and-doesnt-pay-u-s-income-tax/

[104]   Wyden, R. (2015). 10 Ways the Tax System is Unfair to Middle-Class Americans | U.S. Senator Ron Wyden of Oregon.
       •Retrieved from Communications Office website: https://www.wyden.senate.gov/news/blog/post/10-ways-the-tax-system-is-unfair-to-middle-class-americans

[105]   Sforza, T. (2009, September 17). Where do your sales tax dollars actually go? The Orange County Register.
       •Retrieved from https://www.ocregister.com/2009/09/17/where-do-your-sales-tax-dollars-actually-go/

[106]   Christopher, B. (2017, July 25). Here's the most detailed visual of the California budget we know of | CALmatters.
       •Retrieved from https://calmatters.org/articles/california-state-budget-best-visualization-tool/

[107]   Karlamangla, S. (2017, January 16). 13.5 million Californians are covered by Medi-Cal. Here's how Trump's plan could cost the state—Los Angeles Times.
       •Retrieved from http://www.latimes.com/local/politics/la-me-medi-cal-trump-20170116-story.html

[108]   U.S. Census Bureau. (2017). Public education finances: 2015 (G15-ASPEF).
       •Retrieved from Educational Finance Branch website: https://www.census.gov/content/dam/Census/library/publications/2017/econ/g15-aspef.pdf

[109]   Hill, L., Warren, P., Murphy, P., Ugo, I., & Pathak, A. (2016, November). Special Education Finance in California.
       •Retrieved from http://www.ppic.org/content/pubs/report/R_1116LHR.pdf

CHAPTER 9

[110]   Center on Budget and Policy Priorities. (2017, October 10). Policy basics: where do our federal tax dollars go?
       •Retrieved from https://www.cbpp.org/research/federal-budget/policy-basics-where-do-our-federal-tax-dollars-go

[111]   The World Bank. (2017). Fertility rate, total (births per woman) | Data.
       •Retrieved from https://data.worldbank.org/indicator/SP.DYN.TFRT.IN?locations=US

[112]   Population Pyramids of the World from 1950 to 2100. (2017).
       •Retrieved from https://www.populationpyramid.net/united-states-of-america/1950/

[113]   The United States Social Security Administration. (2005). Social Security: A Brief History (No. 21-059).
       •Retrieved from https://www.ssa.gov/history/pdf/2005pamphlet.pdf

[114]   Historical FICA tax information. (n.d.).
       •Retrieved from http://www.milefoot.com/math/businessmath/taxes/fica.htm

[115] United States Census Bureau. (2015). 21.3% of US Participates in Government Assistance
       Programs Each Month (CB15-97).
       •Retrieved from census bureau website: https://www.census.gov/newsroom/press-
       releases/2015/cb15-97.html

[116] U.S. Department of Agriculture. (2018). Supplemental nutrition assistance program.
       •Retrieved from https://fns-prod.azureedge.net/sites/default/files/resource-files/SNAPsummary-
       7.pdf

[117] Statista. (2012, January). U.S. government spending for SNAP benefits (Food Stamps) 1995–2020
       | Statistic.
       •Retrieved from https://www.statista.com/statistics/223080/government -spending-for-snap-
       benefits/

[118] Medicaid.gov. (2018). Medicaid & CHIP enrollment data highlights.
       •Retrieved from https://www.medicaid.gov/medicaid/program-information/medicaid-and-chip-
       enrollment-data/report-highlights/index.html

[119] Statista. (2017). Total Medicaid expenditure from 1966 to 2017.
       •Retrieved from https://www.statista.com/statistics/245348/total-medicaid-expenditure-since-1966/

[120] Chantrill, C. (2017). State Welfare Spending Rank for 2017—Charts.
       •Retrieved from https://www.usgovernmentspending.com/compare_state_spending_2017b40a

[121] Bloom, D., & Manpower Demonstration Research Corporation. (2002). Welfare time limits: State
       policies, implementation, and effects on families. New York City: Manpower Demonstration
       Research Corporation.

[122] Baetjer, H. (2016, August 24). The Welfare Cliff and Why Many Low-Income Workers Will Never
       Overcome Poverty.
       •Retrieved from http://www.learnliberty.org/blog/the-welfare-cliff-and-why-many-low-income-
       workers-will-never-overcome-poverty/

[123] ITM Trading. (2017, July 5). Pension crisis—state and local government pensions underfunded
       [Video file].
       •Retrieved from https://www.youtube.com/watch?v=jrC4_PbOnVc&t=582s

[124] Truth in Accounting. (2018, October 31). California's 'surpluses' result in $269.9 billion of debt.
       •Retrieved from https://www.statedatalab.org/

[125] Truth in Accounting. (2016, October 18). Pension database.
       •Retrieved from https://www.statedatalab.org/pension_database/

[126] California Public Employees' Retirement System—CalPERS. (2017). Investment & pension
       funding facts at a glance for fiscal year 2016–17.
       •Retrieved from https://www.calpers.ca.gov/docs/forms-publications/facts-investment-pension-
       funding.pdf

[127] Truth in Accounting. (2018, October 24). Illinois sliding further into debt.
       •Retrieved from https://www.statedatalab.org/state_data_and_comparisons/detail/illinois

[128] Fox Business. (2017, May 16). Are pensions America's next looming crisis? [Video file].
       •Retrieved from https://www.youtube.com/watch?v=2sn4dgR3PP4

[129] Truth in Accounting. (2018, September 13). New York financial breakdown.
       •Retrieved from https://www.statedatalab.org/state_data_and_comparisons/detail/new-york

[130] Federal Reserve Bank of Saint Louis. (2018, September 21). State and local
       governments,excluding employee retirement funds; credit market instruments; liability, level.
       •Retrieved from https://fred.stlouisfed.org/series/SLGSDODNS

CHAPTER 10

[131]   Tepper, T. (2018, July 25). Millennials prefer cash over stocks, and it could cost them millions |
        Bankrate.com.
        •Retrieved from https://www.bankrate.com/investing/financial-security-july-2018/

[132]   TIME. (2009, August 5). Top 10 things you didn't know about money.
        •Retrieved from
        http://content.time.com/time/specials/packages/article/0,28804,1914560_1914558_1914593,00.ht
        ml

[133]   Federal Reserve board. (2019). Currency in circulation: Value.
        •Retrieved from https://www.federalreserve.gov/paymentsystems/coin_currcircvalue.htm

[134]   Washingtons Blog. (2011, August 2). The Average Life Expectancy For A Fiat Currency Is 27
        Years . . . Every 30 To 40 Years The Reigning Monetary System Fails And Has To Be Retooled
        [Web log post].
        •Retrieved from http://georgewashington2.blogspot.com/2011/08/average-life-expectancy-for-
        fiat.html

[135]   Ebay. (2009, October 27). British coins: silver content for bullion buyers.
        •Retrieved from http://www.ebay.com/gds/British-coins-silver-content-for-bullion-buyers-
        /10000000001664130/g.html

[136]   Bureau of Labor Statistics'. (n.d.). CPI inflation calculator.
        •Retrieved from https://data.bls.gov/cgi-bin/cpicalc.pl

CHAPTER 11

[137]   MacDonald, C. (2016, May 19). Detroit population rank is lowest since 1850. The Detroit News.
        •Retrieved from https://www.detroitnews.com/story/news/local/detroit-city/2016/05/19/detroit-
        population-rank-lowest-since/84574198/

[138]   Zillow. (2018, September 30). Detroit home prices & values.
        •Retrieved from https://www.zillow.com/detroit-mi/home-values/

[139]   Zillow. (2018, September 30). United States home prices & home values.
        •Retrieved from https://www.zillow.com/home-values/

[140]   Spicer, J., & Still, A. (2018, July 23). Poorer Americans buckling as U.S. economy booms.
        •Retrieved from http://fingfx.thomsonreuters.com/gfx/rngs/USA-ECONOMY-
        CONSUMERS/010071CJ2NK/index.html

[141]   Julie Zeveloff, & Gus Lubin. (2012, October 23). The 25 biggest landowners in America.
        •Retrieved from https://www.businessinsider.com/the-25-biggest-landowners-in-america-2012-
        10#5-the-irving-family-owns-12-million-acres-21

[142]   List of US States By Size, In Square Miles. (n.d.).
        •Retrieved from https://state.1keydata.com/states-by-size.php

[143]   Desilver, D. (2015, September 22). The many ways to measure economic inequality.
        •Retrieved from http://www.pewresearch.org/fact-tank/2015/09/22/the-many-ways-to-measure-
        economic-inequality/

[144]   US Census Bureau. (2014). Wealth, Asset Ownership, & Debt of Households Detailed Tables:
        2014.
        •Retrieved from https://www.census.gov/data/tables/2014/demo/wealth/wealth-asset-
        ownership.html

[145]   US Census of Agriculture. (2014). National Agricultural Statistics Service—2012 Census of
        Agriculture—List of Reports and Publications.
        •Retrieved from https://www.nass.usda.gov/Publications/AgCensus/2012/#full_report

[146] Jiang, E. (2018, August 14). The world's largest hedge fund loads up on Alibaba (BABA).
•Retrieved from https://finance.yahoo.com/news/world-largest-hedge-fund-loads-161600060.html

[147] Shen, L. (2018, May 21). Here are the Fortune 500's most valuable companies.
•Retrieved from http://fortune.com/2018/05/21/fortune-500-most-valuable-companies-2018/

[148] Dezember, R. (2018, January 26). My 10-Year odyssey through America's housing crisis.
•Retrieved from https://www.wsj.com/articles/my-10-year-odyssey-through-americas-housing-crisis-1516981725

[149] Maddox. (n.d.). I hope SOPA passes.
•Retrieved from http://thebestpageintheuniverse.net/c.cgi?u=pass_sopa

[150] Propublica. (2017, January 14). Bailout List: Banks, Auto Companies, and More | Eye on the Bailout |.
•Retrieved from https://projects.propublica.org/bailout/list

[151] Sweets, M. (2008). Bailout. In Urban Dictionary.
•Retrieved from http://www.urbandictionary.com/define.php?term=Bailout

[152] Sweet, K. (2017, August 31). Wells Fargo says 3.5 million accounts involved in scandal.
•Retrieved from https://www.apnews.com/c3de75ac78004f04be8291b1b76c2cd0

CHAPTER 12

[153] Quinnipiac University. (2020). QU poll release detail.
•Retrieved from https://poll.qu.edu/national/release-detail?ReleaseID=3654

[154] International Monetary Fund. (2018). Inflation rate, average consumer prices annual percent change.
•Retrieved from https://www.imf.org/external/datamapper/PCPIPCH@WEO/WEOWORLD/VEN

[155] List of countries by personal income tax rate. (n.d.).
•Retrieved from https://tradingeconomics.com/country-list/personal-income-tax-rate

[156] GFP. (2017). Defense Spending by Country.
•Retrieved from https://www.globalfirepower.com/defense-spending-budget.asp

CHAPTER 13

[157] Government historical debt outstanding annual 2000–2018. (n.d.).
•Retrieved from https://www.treasurydirect.gov/govt/reports/pd/histdebt/histdebt_histo5.htm

[158] International Monetary Fund. (2017). Real GDP Growth Annual Percent Change.
•Retrieved from http://www.imf.org/external/datamapper/NGDP_RPCH@WEO/OEMDC/ADVEC/WEOWORLD

[159] Hanke, S., & Krus, N. (2012, September 26). Hanke-Krus Hyperinflation Table.
•Retrieved from https://www.cato.org/sites/cato.org/files/pubs/pdf/hanke-krus-hyperinflation-table-may-2013.pdf

[160] Marcuse, H. (2018, October 7). Historical US Dollars to German marks currency conversion.
•Retrieved from http://www.history.ucsb.edu/faculty/marcuse/projects/currency.htm

CHAPTER 14

[161] Iskyan, K. (2016, May 17). Here's the story of how the Hunt brothers tried to corner the silver market.
•Retrieved from https://www.businessinsider.com/hunt-brothers-trying-to-corner-silver-market-2016-5

[162] Rhyne, D. (2016, February 13). History of gold-silver ratio.
•Retrieved from https://www.youshouldbuygold.com/history-of-gold-silver-ratio/

[163] Silver to Gold Ratio Historical Timeline (1883 to 2009) | Silver Investments | Silver Coins [Video file]. (2012, November 10).
•Retrieved from https://www.youtube.com/watch?v=CidFKAeB9tU

[164] The Silver Institute, & GFMS Thomson Reuters. (2017). World silver survey 2017.
•Retrieved from http://www.silverinstitute.org/wp-content/uploads/2017/08/WSS2017.pdf

CHAPTER 15

[165] Bloomberg. (2014, October 2). Bill Gates: Bitcoin is exciting because it's cheap.
•Retrieved from https://www.bloomberg.com/news/videos/2014-10-02/bill-gates-bitcoin-is-exciting-because-its-cheap

[166] $1mn by 2020: John McAfee will still 'eat his own d*ck? if he's wrong about Bitcoin. (2017, November 30).
•Retrieved from https://www.rt.com/news/411379-john-mcafee-bitcoin-prediction/

[167] Bank Of America. (n.d.). Wire Transfer—International Wire Transfers from Bank of America.
•Retrieved from https://www.bankofamerica.com/foreign-exchange/wire-transfer.go

[168] Papadimitriou, O. (2009, April 2). How credit card transaction processing works: steps, fees & participants.
•Retrieved from https://wallethub.com/edu/credit-card-transaction/25511/

[169] Popken, B. (2017, July 13). Visa offers restaurants $10,000 to go cashless in 'war on cash'.
•Retrieved from https://www.nbcnews.com/business/consumer/war-cash-intensifies-visa-offers-restaurants-10-000-go-cashless-n782276

[170] HuffPost. (2013, February 4). Canada discontinues the penny.
•Retrieved from https://www.huffingtonpost.com/2013/02/04/canadian-penny-discontinued_n_2615919.html

[171] About the IMF. (n.d.).
•Retrieved from https://www.imf.org/en/About

[172] International Monetary Fund. (2018, November 13). Winds of change: the case for new digital currency.
•Retrieved from https://www.imf.org/en/News/Articles/2018/11/13/sp111418-winds-of-change-the-case-for-new-digital-currency

[173] Wile, R. (2013, December 10). 927 People Own Half Of All Bitcoins.
•Retrieved from http://www.businessinsider.com/927-people-own-half-of-the-bitcoins-2013-12

[174] CNN. (2014, February 27). Yellen: Fed can't regulate Bitcoin [Video file].
•Retrieved from https://www.youtube.com/watch?v=d-vTleht5Hw

CHAPTER 16

[175] Investopedia. (2018, September 14). Q Ratio (Tobin's Q Ratio).
•Retrieved from https://www.investopedia.com/terms/q/qratio.asp

[176] Mislinski, J. (2018, November 2). The Q ratio and market valuation: October update.
•Retrieved from https://www.advisorperspectives.com/dshort/updates/2018/11/02/the-q-ratio-and-market-valuation-october-update

[177] Grant Cardone. (2018, July 2). Leverage your real estate—real estate investing made simple[Video file].
•Retrieved from https://www.youtube.com/watch?v=oAUKFNJ8qYk&t=885s

[178] Meet Kevin. (2018, August 13). Grant Cardone will NEVER show you This [Video file].
•Retrieved from
https://www.youtube.com/watch?v=qAa5hu6_6jg&fbclid=IwAR0KYdIWYNTzo6zbBET5qoS7Uyi9st
p-h9h8qI9DWIt30T-rDprAG-BIeW4&app=desktop

[179] McAlvany Financial. (2017, November 7). US margin debt hitting all time highs, borrowing to
speculate has never been more popular [Video file].
•Retrieved from https://www.youtube.com/watch?v=IBj3qoLuIQE&t=

[180] Mislinski, J. (2018, October 23). Margin debt and the market—dshort.
•Retrieved from https://www.advisorperspectives.com/dshort/updates/2018/10/23/margin-debt-and-
the-market

[181] Kingsley, P. (2017, November 25). How credit ratings agencies rule the world.
•Retrieved from https://www.theguardian.com/business/2012/feb/15/credit-ratings-agencies-
moodys

CHAPTER 17

[182] Byrnes, B. (2013, February 28). Seth Godin: "we're flying too low".
•Retrieved from https://www.fool.com/investing/general/2013/02/28/seth-godin-were-flying-too-
low.aspx